St. Louis Community
College

Library

5801 Wilson Avenue
St. Louis, Missouri 63110

BRO
DART

PRINTED IN U.S.A.

23-263-002

Tennessee
Strings

Tennessee Strings

The Story

of Country Music

in Tennessee

BY CHARLES K. WOLFE

PUBLISHED IN COOPERATION WITH

The Tennessee Historical Commission

THE UNIVERSITY OF TENNESSEE PRESS

KNOXVILLE

TENNESSEE THREE STAR BOOKS / *Paul H. Bergeron, General Editor*

This series of general-interest books about significant Tennessee topics is sponsored jointly by the Tennessee Historical Commission and the University of Tennessee Press. Inquiries about manuscripts should be addressed to Professor Bergeron, History Department, University of Tennessee, Knoxville.

Copyright © 1977 by the University of Tennessee Press.
Manufactured in the United States of America.

Library of Congress Cataloging in Publication Data
Wolfe, Charles K.
  Tennessee strings.
  (Tennessee three star books)
  Bibliography: p.
  Includes index.
  1. Country music—Tennessee—History and criticism.
  2. Tennessee—History. I. Title. II. Series
ML3561.C69W64   784   77–8052
ISBN 0–87049–224–1

Representative selections by many of the early artists discussed in Tennessee Strings *are available on an LP album produced by Rounder Records in conjunction with this book. The album also is entitled* Tennessee Strings *(Rounder LP 1030,* available from Rounder Records, 186 Willow Ave., Somerville, Mass.).

ABOUT THE AUTHOR

Charles Wolfe comes from an Ozark family of fiddlers and pickers, but his serious interest in the study of folk and country music dates from his graduate-school days at the University of Kansas. Since joining the faculty of Middle Tennessee State University, Murfreesboro, in 1970, Professor Wolfe has actively furthered this interest through research, production of recordings of folk musicians, coordination of folk festivals, writing and editing, and counseling others on folklore projects. He has written extensively on folklore and popular culture both in articles and in books, having contributed chapters to the new *Illustrated History of Country Music* (Doubleday) and authored *Grand Ole Opry: The Early Years* 1925–1935 (*Old Time Music*).

To my daughters, Stacey and Cindy

Preface

Like jazz, country music is a unique American art form that began as regional folk art. It spoke to the people of the rural South, helping them to come to grips with the traumatic changes of the modern age: to meet the challenges to traditional values posed by industrialization and "progress." Country music, which is one of the most popular and influential manifestations of southern culture, grew up in several key centers around the nation during the first half of this century: Atlanta, the first country recording center; Chicago, home of one of the first successful country radio shows; southern California, home of the singing cowboys; and most recently Austin, Texas, home of the "cosmic cowboy" and "outlaw" country music. While each of these centers has had its day, only one area has remained constantly in the forefront of the music's development: Tennessee.

As country music grew up in Tennessee, it drew from sources as diverse as the rural ballads and fiddle music, the church music of the country singing conventions, and the black music of the southwestern delta area. As country music was commercialized through radio and recordings, Tennessee was soon recognized as a national center for the music. Early record companies came into the Tennessee mountains to record native talent on location, and radio stations in Nashville, Knoxville, and Chattanooga achieved most of their early success by broadcasting local country talent. After World War II, Nashville, with its Grand Ole Opry, became the economic and creative axis for a music that achieved worldwide popularity and significance.

The story of country music in Tennessee is by no means the full story; that has been told elsewhere, in studies much larger than this. But there is an important rationale for looking at this music from a regional perspective. More than any other art form, country music thrives on constant communication between its audience and its performers, and between popular and traditional folk cultures. One cannot pretend to understand the music without understanding the social context that produced it and maintained it. And this context seems most easily and obviously defined in terms of geography. After all, the musicians in a given area knew each other, played with each other, worked with each other, exchanged tunes and ideas, and shared notions of what their music was all about. This was especially true in the formative years of country music, when travel was hard, communication was difficult, and most music was heard live. But even when mass media—radio and records—broke down the geographical isolation within the state, a new social context emerged in Nashville, where hundreds of influential musicians with access to mass media gathered. Context is thus important to understanding both the folk aspect of the music—the mountains and the country—and the pop aspect, the Nashville scene. Musicians outside of Nashville have been influenced by what they hear on radio and records, and the music played in Nashville has been influenced by the styles and songs people bring to town. New songs are played and sung in old ways, and old songs and new styles are molded into new ways.

Tennessee has been country music's best environment because Tennessee has been able to maintain both of these cultures, the pop and the traditional. Within thirty minutes' travel from the slick, ultramodern studios of Nashville, one can still find old banjo pickers playing rags they learned from their fathers during World War I. It is this richness and this diversity, and its complex interaction, that justifies a study of country music in Tennessee.

CHARLES K. WOLFE

January 1977
Murfreesboro, Tennessee

Contents

Preface   *page vii*
1. The Folk Background   *3*
2. Out of the Hills: The First Professionals   *27*
3. George Hay and the Grand Ole Opry   *54*
4. Honky-tonk, Tuxedoes, and Bluegrass   *75*
5. Nashville Skyline   *93*
    Selected Resources on Country Music   *112*
    Index   *114*

ILLUSTRATIONS

"The Source of Country Music"   *front cover*
Sheet Music for "Kittie Wells"; "Ballet cards"   *page 9*
Knoxville Harmony; example of shape notes   *13*
Rural fiddlers   *16*
Market House fiddlers, *c.* 1886   *21*
Taylor brothers' "War of the Roses"   *24*
Advertisement for crystal set   *29*
Fiddlin' John Carson and Uncle Am Stuart   *31*
Aeolian Vocalion record cover, 1927   *34*
Sam McGee and Uncle Dave Macon   *37*
Mountain City fiddlers' convention, 1925   *38 & 39*
Uncle Dave Macon; Charlie Bowman and Ralph Peer   *45*
Tennessee Ramblers, 1929; a Vaughan songbook   *51*
Uncle Jimmy Thompson; George Hay; old Studio A   *57*
Bate's Possum Hunters, 1926, 1928   *62*
DeFord Bailey   *65*
The Gully Jumpers; Opry's first tour group   *68*
Dixieliners' string band; Roy Acuff's band, 1938   *71*
Minnie Pearl on tour; Ernie Ford; Eddy Arnold   *79*

Singer Redd Stewart; Bill Monroe and band   *83*
Cas Walker's band; Chet Atkins and group   *87*
WOPI control room; "Saturday Night Jamboree"   *89*
Jim Stanton and the Bailey Brothers   *91*
Paul Cohen; Steve Scholes; Fred Rose; Owen Bradley   *95*
Selection of Nashville's independent record labels   *98*
Chet Atkins and Merle Travis; Ryman Auditorium   *102*
Sun Records' cover, featuring Elvis Presley   *106*
Woodland studio control room; Nitty Gritty Dirt Band   *108*
Buck dancing and spoon playing at Clarksville   *110*

Illustration credits: Author's collection, pages 9 (bottom), 29, 45 (right), 98, 106, 110; Alcyone Bate Beasley, pages 62, 68 (bottom); Mrs. Bryan Boyd, page 21 (top); Mrs. Henry Brown, page 87 (top); Staley M. Cain, pages 31, 45 (bottom left), 89 (bottom); Country Music Foundation Library and Media Center, front cover, pages 57 (top right and bottom), 65, 68, (top), 71, 79, 83, 87 (bottom), 95, 102, 108; Claude Grant, page 89 (top); Mrs. Mildred Hatcher, pages 38–39; Dick Hulan, page 16; George Pullen Jackson Collection, Department of Special Collections, University of California at Los Angeles, page 13; Jack Jackson, page 51 (bottom right); Leona Jackson and Rounder Records, page 91; Sam McGee, page 37; Arch Macon, page 45 (top); Herb Peck, page 21 (bottom); Mrs. Willie Sharp, page 51 (top); Tennessee State Library and Archives, pages 9 (top), 26; Mrs. Katherine Thompson, page 57 (top left).

Tennessee
Strings

1. The Folk Background

On August 30, 1916, an Englishman named Cecil Sharp arrived in the mountain community of Rocky Fork, Tennessee. Newspapers in the larger cities on that day were full of stories of the Great War and of the upcoming election between Woodrow Wilson ("He kept us out of war") and Charles Evans Hughes. Advertisements hailed the virtues of Henry Ford's revolutionary Model T, the "tin lizzie"; Americans were traveling more and more by car in August 1916, but most people still had to put up their cars in the winter and fall back on the dependable horse and buggy. Many Americans were worried about the war in Europe, and whether the country would be drawn into it. Others worried about the ominous troop build-up along the Mexican border. But these worries seemed remote in Rocky Fork. Located in tiny Unicoi County, on the Tennessee–North Carolina border, Rocky Fork was sheltered from the world by the imposing bulk of the Bald Mountains to the east and of Sugar Loaf Knob to the south and west. The community was not easily accessible, even in 1916; most outsiders coming into the community were missionaries or hunters. Cecil Sharp was a little of both: he was a hunter, but he was hunting songs, not game.

Sharp had begun his journey to remote sections of the Appalachians in July 1916 on the suggestion of a correspondent in Kentucky who claimed that, because of the isolation of these mountain communities, old English folk songs were still being sung much as they had been sung by the original English and Scottish settlers in the eighteenth and nineteenth centuries. Thus, working with the Presbyterian Missionary Board, the scholarly, polite Englishman and his fellow music student and traveling companion, Miss Maud Karpeles, had spent their first month in Madison and Buncombe counties of North Carolina. Now, they had come due north to the other side of the Smoky Mountains to begin yet another round of introductions and interviews among the singers in the community.

Sharp's habit was to spend a week or ten days in a community, visiting all the singers who were within walking distance. He listened to the songs of mountain men and women, transcribing the music on a pad he carried, while Maud Karpeles noted the words in shorthand. When he arrived at Rocky Fork, Sharp had already found over 100 old songs. After resting for a day, Sharp and Miss Karpeles set out for the nearby community of Flag Pond, where some interviews had been arranged. Soon after arriving there, Sharp met Mr. and Mrs. James Gabriel Coates, who were known locally as singers. For two days the Coateses sang for Sharp, and he knew at once that he had indeed found "old songs." Mrs. Coates sang numbers with titles like "The Sheffield Apprentice" and "Little Musgrave and Lady Barnard." One of her favorites was a tune Sharp knew as "The Gypsy Laddie," and he listened closely as Mrs. Coates sang it:

It was late in the night when the squire came home,
Enquiring for his lady;
His servant made a sure reply;
She's gone with the gypsen Davy.
Chorus: Rattle-tum a-gypsen-gypsen,
Rattle-tum a-gypsen Davy.

O go catch up my milk-white steed,
He's black and then he's speedy.
I'll ride all night till broad daylight,
Or overtake my lady.

He rode and he rode till he came to the town,
And he rode till he came to Barley.
And tears came rolling down his cheeks
And there he spied his lady.

O come, go back, my own true love,
O come, go back, my honey.
I'll lock you up in the chamber so high
Where the gypsens can't come round you.

I won't come back, your own true love,
Nor I won't come back your honey.
I wouldn't give a kiss from gypsen's lips
For all your land and money.

She soon run through her gay clothing,
Her velvet shoes and stockings;
Her gold ring off her finger was gone
And the gold plate off her bosom.

O once I had a house and land,
Feather-bed and money,
But now I've come to an old straw pad
With the gypsens all around me.

Reviewing his notes that night, Sharp had reason to be satisfied. He knew of numerous versions of "The Gypsy Laddie" that had been collected years before in England and Scotland. The song had been printed as early as 1740; it had been sung in Ireland in 1860; it was apparently sung during the Revolutionary War by British soldiers stationed in Long Island. Now Sharp was finding it still being sung in the mountains of East Tennessee. Nor was Mrs. Coates's love of the song unique or unusual; before Sharp left Rocky Fork he collected two more versions of the song from women in the area.

In many ways "The Gypsy Laddie" was typical of the old ballads Sharp was finding. It was old and traceable back over 200 years into the history of Scotland and England. It was a ballad—a song that told a story and emphasized the events of the story more than the singer's feelings about them. It contained, as did many such ballads, stanzas which represented dialogue of the characters. It utilized "nonsense phrases," such as the "Rattle-tum a-gypsen-gypsen" in the chorus, and "stock phrases" which were traditional clichés found in many ballads. Phrases like "milk-white steed" and "up in the chamber so high" had little practical reference for Appalachian hill country folk, but the phrases were preserved in the old songs, along with English place names and references to nobility. And, finally, "The Gypsy Laddie" told a story about basic, elemental concerns: love, wealth, sadness. These elemental concerns had helped give the song wide appeal and had helped keep it alive for so many years.

Cecil Sharp could not know, of course, but the songs he collected from hill country people in the World War I years were the ancestors of modern country music. In fact, "The Gypsy Laddie" shares many of the qualities of the modern Nashville country lament. It is about marriage problems; it describes one spouse running away from the other and then regretting the break. It contains the motifs of lost love and the fall from wealth to poverty. It has a sad ending. It reflects the romantic appeal of the rebel, the rambler—in this case, the gypsy—but in modern country music, the central character could be the trucker, the rodeo cowboy, the outlaw, or even the musician. A close look at "The Gypsy Laddie" reveals the folk roots of much modern country music and suggests surprising connections between the slickly packaged music product of today's multimillion-dollar Grand Ole Opry House and the simple, unadorned ballads of the Scottish and English peasants. It was curiously symbolic that Sharp reported later that, in order to get his informants to sing the old ballads he wanted, he had to ask for " 'love-songs,' which is their name for these ditties." The definition of "love song" is in some ways remarkably unchanged in modern country music.

For some years before Sharp went into the Appalachians, scholars in

England and America had been aware of the history and significance of folk songs. But most of the study of folk song in the nineteenth century had been done by armchair collectors who worked in libraries, combing old books and magazines for song texts. Sharp was one of the first scholars to go out and collect songs directly from the people, to show that the songs were "on the ground," actively sung and very much a part of the folk culture. (He was also one of the first to collect the music to the songs, as opposed to just the words.) When his collection was published, first in 1917 and then in an expanded form in 1932, the book helped to popularize the notion that the southern Appalachians, because the natives were so isolated, was a rare and unique source for these old songs. Sharp went on to collect more old songs in North Carolina, Kentucky, and Virginia than he did in Tennessee, yet most people saw Sharp's sources not in particular states but rather simply in "the southern mountains." Actually, the old songs Sharp found were not unique to the area, nor was the area so isolated as popular conception supposed. Later collectors found old English songs in many different areas across the country, from New England to Mississippi. And the railroad, the steamboat, and industry had for some years before 1916 been breaking down the isolation and "purity" of mountain culture. Nevertheless the popular image of the southern mountains as a prime source of folk songs was formed (and still holds today), and this image was to have much to do with the later commercial development of this folk music. Tennessee especially benefited from this image when radio and phonograph records came along; recording sessions were held in Tennessee because the northern recording executives thought old songs could best be found in the mountains, and the founder of the Grand Ole Opry chose Tennessee because he felt the hill country music would be most authentic there. And the music, to be sure, was indeed present in the mountains.

Collectors generally classify ballads into two types: those originating in England or Scotland are often referred to as Child ballads (in honor of Francis Child, who made a definitive early collection of them), while those originating in America are often classified with a system devised by another collector, Malcolm Laws. A survey of one of the largest collections of Tennessee folk songs—that of Professor George Boswell, which contains some 770 texts— shows that the ten most common Child ballads found in the United States as a whole are also the ten most found in Tennessee; in both cases the most popular old English song is the well-known "Barbara Allen." But overall, only about 10 percent of the song texts in the Boswell collection are Child ballads; many of the rest are genuinely old songs, but songs with less impressive pedigrees. They include native American ballads (rather similar to the British ballads, except that American ballads often include a "moral" to be learned as a result of the sad story), comic and nonsense songs, sentimental songs (often about home, mother, death, or children—or all four), play-party songs and children's songs (often sung by children to accompany games), and songs borrowed from black traditions. A surprising number of cowboy songs show up in later statewide collections of Tennessee folk songs. Religious songs also played a large role in the vocal tradition.

Where did these other types of song come from? Many of the singers did in fact learn their songs orally (and aurally) from other singers in their family or community. An analysis of Boswell's collection of Tennessee folk songs (many of which were collected in the 1940s and 1950s) reveals that over half of the songs were learned from relatives, usually the mother or the father. Yet in many cases of oral transmission, print helped out the process; many old ballad singers possessed handwritten texts, or "ballets," of their songs. Sometimes these ballets were collected and pasted or copied into books which were passed down through the family. There have been few instances of any singers actually singing from these ballets, but these texts were available for reference if need be. The origins of some folk songs collected in Tennessee have been traced to the popular music of the nineteenth century. From before the Civil War, America had a thriving "Tin Pan Alley" song-writing industry, grinding out songs for use in minstrel shows, vaudeville, and theater. A "hit" song in the nineteenth century was defined through its success in sheet music publication, and apparently many of these pieces of sheet music made their way into the rural South. Someone who had a piano and could read music would play the song, teach it to a second person who, like many hill people, had no piano, and he in turn would teach it orally to yet a third. As the song circulated through countless hands over the decades, its origins and its author were soon forgotten; it became simply an old song learned orally from an earlier generation. It became a folk song. Thus "Wildwood Flower," one of the most popular folk songs found in Tennessee, can be traced back to an 1860 song by Maud Irving and J. P. Webster, "I'll Twine Mid the Ringlets." "Kitty Wells," popular in Middle Tennessee, was published in sheet music in 1861.

Some singers, of course, did compose original material. In addition to the older folk ballads, England for hundreds of years had seen a tradition of the "broadside" ballad: a song composed about some topical event and sold in the streets on roughly printed sheets of paper. This tradition, too, was brought to the United States and formed the basis for most of the early original, composed songs. Sometimes called "event songs," these compositions chronicled such current events as train wrecks, sensational murders, mining disasters, famous crimes (and criminals), death of prominent people, and many other happenings that interested rural southerners. Many of the songs lingered in tradition long after the events themselves were forgotten. A song usually told about the event—giving date, place, and often gruesome detail—and concluded with a moral to be drawn from it all. Like their British counterparts, these songs were frequently sold in printed form by their makers or singers. In the Kentucky–Tennessee area many of the songs were printed on small cards about the size of a post card (still called "ballet cards" by old-timers), usually signed by the composer or singer; rural minstrels wandered through the mountains singing at rural courthouses and making some money by selling their ballet cards for a penny or a nickel each. These minstrels were probably the first professional (or semiprofessional) musicians of country music; many of them were blind, and music was the only way for them to earn their living. Very little is known about these minstrels, but they obviously played a major role in transmitting songs and singing styles from one community to another.

One such minstrel was Charles Oaks. Oaks was a blind musician who was born possibly in Richmond, Kentucky, but who spent most of his life playing throughout eastern Tennessee. He was composing event songs and singing event songs shortly after the turn of the century, and from 1900 to 1930 he was a familiar figure at county fairs, picnics, political events, and on street corners. He often played at train stations in Knoxville for nickels and dimes, where he influenced a number of local musicians. A couple of examples of broadside ballet cards by Oaks have survived, and they are probably typical of the genre. One is entitled "The Southern Railroad Wreck, Which Occurred Near New Market, Tennessee, September 1904," and is a rather long, detailed account of a major railroad tragedy in East Tennessee in which over seventy passengers were killed. The text, which is too long to quote in full here, contains some rather grisly details: "One dying woman prayed to live, / Just for her children dear; / A headless woman's body lay there, / Her head was lying near." The last stanza concludes with the admonition that when we board a railroad train "It's little do we know; / That we may meet the same sad fate, / And into eternity go." Because Oaks's career extended up into the 1930s and because he was one of the few old minstrels to make records, a little is known about his singing style: he sang in a high, strained tenor voice suggestive of that of later East Tennessee singers like Roy Acuff,

This original sheet music for "Kittie Wells," one of many 19-century pop songs that entered folk tradition, was issued in 1861. Below are "ballet cards," which minstrels like blind Dick Burnett from southern Kentucky peddled for a penny or a nickel each in the days before radio and records.

Kittie Wells.

Composed by T. BRIGHAM BISHOP.

Moderato con Express.

1. You ask what makes this dar-kie
2. I nev - er shall for-get the
3. I oft - en wish that I was

weep,.................. Why, he like oth-ers am not gay;.................. What
day, ... That we to-geth-er roam'd the dells;.................. I
dead,.................. And laid be-side her in the tomb,.................. The

---

GOING AROUND THE WORLD

I'm going across the ocean friend of mine,
I'm going across the ocean friend of mine
I'm going across the ocean if I don't change my notion.
I'm going around the world friend of mine
I'll write my girl a letter friend of mine
I'll write my girl a letter friend of mine
I'll write my girl a letter friend of mine and I'll write my girl a letter and I'll tell her that she'd better
For I'm going around the world friend of mine.
Oh! Come and sit by me girl O mine
Come and sit down by me girl O mine,
Come and sit down by me, say you love no one but me, and we'll go around this world friend O mine
Oh, give to me your hand girl 'O mine,
Oh! give to me your hand girl 'O mine,
Oh! give to me your hand, Say you love no other man, And we'll go around the world, Girl 'O mine.
I may cross the sea girl of mine
I may cross the sea girl of mine.
I may cross the sea.
Oh! come and go with me, I'm going around the world girl of mine
I'm going around the world friend of mine
I'm going around the world friend of mine
I've been around the world, with a banjo picking girl, I've been around the world friend of mine
—: Composed By
R. D. BURNETT
Monticello, Ky.

ARE YOU HAPPY OR LONESOME

Come back to me in my dreaming,
Come back to me once more,
Come with love light gleaming, as in days of yore,
I wonder if you want me, or if your heart is still true,
When the spring roses are blooming, I'll come back to you.
Some where a heart is breaking calling me back to you,
Memories of love are waiting each happy home I knew,
Absence makes my heart fonder, is it the same with you,
Are you still happy I wonder or do you feel lonesome too.
If you thought I was lonesome would you come back to me,
You were my one and only one in the days that used to be.
Absence makes my heart fonder, is it the same with you,
Are you still happy I wonder or do you feel lonesome too.
When the sun is sinking in the golden west
When the birds and flowers they have gone to rest,
Come tell me that you love me and if your heart is still true.
When the Spring roses are blooming I'll come back to you.
BURNETT & RUTHERFORD.

and he deliberately paced his performance to make sure his words could be clearly understood. Obviously the words to a broadside song would be of major importance, and Oaks was probably typical in his concern for them. Other songs in his repertoire dealt with early-twentieth-century regional events, such as the Scopes trial (held in 1925 in nearby Dayton, Tennessee), Floyd Collins, William Jennings Bryan, and such national events as the Great War and the sinking of the Titanic. In some cases, minstrels like Oaks may have really acted as news carriers through their topical songs, but in most cases they probably catered to the fascination that people have with major tragedies or controversies and the desire to talk about them. Although few of Oaks's printed ballets survived, some of the songs he (and those like him) sung were preserved in oral tradition.

The nineteenth-century ballad singer, whether he was singing the old ballads from England, old ballads from America, or more recent broadside ballads, often sang unaccompanied. Today the public is accustomed to seeing even the most serious folk singer perform with at least the guitar, but the guitar was not really known much in Tennessee until the era following World War I. Cecil Sharp reported, in 1917, that "I came across but one singer who sang to an instrumental accompaniment"; virtually all of his informants sang without accompaniment. This a cappella style also gave the singers a certain freedom in timing; Sharp noticed "the habit of dwelling arbitrarily upon certain notes of the melody, generally the weaker accents," which helped break up the "monotonous regularity of the phrasing." (This type of improvisational freedom, which is today associated most often with the blues, is seldom apparent in modern country music; the steady beat generated by the guitar works against it.) Another freedom of solo singing style was the use of the "gapped" scale, where singers sang in scales containing only five or six notes to the octave instead of the customary seven.

With the exception of blind minstrels like Charlie Oaks, few of the mountain ballad singers were in any way professional. However, exceptional singers (usually those who knew a large number of songs) had a certain amount of prestige in their community. As late as 1961, when folklorist Sandy Paton was researching in East Tennessee, he was told by the operator of a general store: "You ought to go up and see Abe Trivett. Forty years ago, up in the logging camps, whenever we wanted music, we'd holler for old Abe." After forty years, the reputation of ballad singer Abe Trivett still survived in the community. His case is probably typical.

In 1951 Maud Karpeles, Sharp's assistant in his earlier research, returned to the Appalachians with a recording machine to revisit some of the families she had visited with Sharp. She noted:

I found, as I had been led to expect, that mountain life has been completely revolutionized during the last twenty to twenty-five years. Roads and electricity have brought "civilization" to the mountains. The roads have made markets accessible and the people are now so busy making money in order to buy electric appliances and to improve the general material standard of life that they no longer have the leisure that they formerly possessed. The radio, which now operates in nearly every mountain home, has let loose a flood of "hill-billy" and other popular music, and this is gradually submerging the traditional songs.

The attitude of Maud Karpeles echoes that of many older folklorists: that "hill-billy" music was some culture from "outside" that was foisted on the people of the South, displacing the more genuine folk songs. Many today would argue that the hillbilly music coming from radios in mountain cabins was simply a commercialized development of the musical ideas found in the old ballads and "love songs." In 1951 Maud Karpeles, furthermore, was able to record over ninety songs "traditional" enough to suit even her standards; the fact that these older songs existed side by side with the newer hillbilly styles might have suggested to Maud Karpeles that she was dealing with one type of music, not two.

One type of song Sharp did not try to collect in his journeys into the mountains was the religious folk song. Had he done so, he would have found a thriving tradition of religious singing, not only in the mountains but across rural Tennessee. The documentation of this complex tradition was left to pioneer Tennessee folklorist George Pullen Jackson, whose 1932 study *White Spirituals in the Southern Uplands* traced for the first time the history and scope of religious folk music. For generations of southern folk musicians, church and church-related music provided the initial and, in many cases the only, opportunity to sing. Throughout the nineteenth century "singing conventions" were held annually or quarterly in courthouse squares or churches across the South; people gathered to sing the old songs, visit, and enjoy "dinner on the ground." What music education most rural southerners had came from "singing schools," where a self-styled "singing master" came into the community and organized a singing class running usually from two to three weeks. At first these schools were conducted strictly on a subscription basis, but later, in the early twentieth century, some of them were sponsored by local churches and even by song book publishers. Pupils were taught the "rudiments" of music: how to read notes, mark time (often taught by encouraging pupils to slap the desk with their hands), and sing parts. A surprising amount of the singing techniques and harmony styles of these old gospel traditions were to find their way into country music.

Much of the early singing was congregational singing done from songbooks with shape notes: notes where pitch is indicated by shape rather than position on the staff. Such singing was called "fasola" singing for two reasons: The old singers often started songs by singing note names instead of words, and, instead of the modern scale names (*do re mi fa sol la ti do*), the older singers knew only four names, *fa sol la* and an occasional *mi* thrown in. They sang the scale as: *fa sol la fa sol la mi fa*. Songbooks using this simplified notation originated in New England in the early 1700s and peaked in popularity from 1770 to 1800; by 1853, one eastern musician declared that the shape notes, or "buckwheat notes," were all but extinct except in a few isolated places in the West.

Such was not the case. The songs, and their shape-note system of notation, had moved into the South, where they continued to flourish. Rural singing masters across the South compiled books of songs with four-shape notation, borrowing some songs from earlier books, composing others, and "arranging" yet others from songs sung locally in oral tradition. These songbooks were published and they in turn provided material for yet others; sometimes song authors were given credit, sometimes not. The books themselves were generally wider than they were tall, contained anywhere from a hundred to several hundred sacred songs, and were usually prefaced by instructions on the "rudiments" of fasola singing. Between 1815 and 1855 over twenty of these songbooks were published throughout the South; two of the earliest were *Western Harmony* (1824), published in the then-village of Nashville, and *Columbian Harmony* (1825), compiled by William Moore, from Wilson County, Tennessee. Some of these songbooks were kept in families for generations, long after they had gone out of print; and many singers knew their songs so well they did not need a book.

Two other important songbooks of the old four-shape notations reflected the popularity of this singing style in Tennessee in the first half of the nineteenth century: Caldwell's *Union Harmony* (1837), published at Maryville, Tennessee, and Jackson's *Knoxville Harmony* (1838), published in Madisonville, Tennessee. But by far the most popular four-shape songbook was the book which gave its name to an entire style of singing: White and King's *Sacred Harp* (1844). The *Sacred Harp* was published in Georgia and reflected the fact that Georgia and Alabama were major centers of this sort of

The thriving tradition of gospel singing made an early contribution to country music. Illustrated here are the title page from Jackson's Knoxville Harmony, *published in Madisonville, 1838 (top), and a selection from that book, "The Good Old Way," showing the shape note convention.*

THE KNOXVILLE HARMONY

OF

MUSIC MADE EASY,

WHICH IS AN INTERESTING SELECTION OF

HYMNS AND PSALMS,

USUALLY SUNG IN CHURCHES:

SELECTED FROM THE BEST AUTHORS IN GENERAL USE.

ALSO,

A VARIETY OF ANTHEMS;

TO WHICH IS ADDED,

A NUMBER OF ORIGINAL TUNES;

BEING ENTIRELY NEW, AND WELL ADAPTED FOR THE USE OF SCHOOLS AND CHURCHES.

COMPOSED BY JOHN B. JACKSON.

TOGETHER WITH A COMPLETE INTRODUCTION TO THE PROPER GROUNDS OF VOCAL MUSIC,
AND RULES WELL EXPLAINED TO BEGINNERS.

D. & M. SHIELDS & CO., AND JOHN B. JACKSON, PROPRIETORS.

MADISONVILLE, TEN.

PRINTED BY A. W. ELDER.

1838.

THE GOOD OLD WAY. L. M.

The queen of the world and the child,

[of the skies]

Lift up your heads, Immanuel's friends,   O halle,   halle - lujah,
And taste the pleasure Jesus   sends,   O halle,   hale - lujah,

Let nothing cause you to delay,   O halle, halle lu jah,   But hasten on the good old way, O halle, halle - lu - jah!

2 Our conflicts here, though great they be,
Shall not prevent our victory,
If we but watch, and strive, and pray,
Like soldiers in the good old way.

CHORUS.
And I'll sing hallelujah,
And glory to God on high;
And I'll sing hallelujah,
There's glory beaming from the sky.

3 O good old way, how sweet thou art!
May none of us from the depart,
But may our actions always say,
We're marching on the good old way,

singing; this book was constantly reprinted and revised until by 1911 it contained over 600 tunes. Indeed, the *Sacred Harp* is still used today by four-note singers across the South; its influence in Tennessee is especially apparent in the southern parts of middle and western Tennessee.

The religious song tradition took a slightly different direction in East Tennessee. By 1832 songbooks using a system of seven shapes—the familiar names of today's scale—were in use in the North, and by 1848 there appeared the first southern seven-shape book, W. H. and M. L. Swan's *Harp of Columbia*, published in Knoxville. This book for years dominated East Tennessee sacred singing, and was second in influence only to the original *Sacred Harp*. Throughout East Tennessee groups of singers using this book called themselves (and still call themselves) ''Harp Singers'' or ''Old Harp Singers,'' and printings of the 1867 revision of the book (entitled *New Harp of Columbia*) have continued well into the modern era. Some of the song titles in the *Harp of Columbia* even bore geographical placenames of East Tennessee: ''Athens,'' ''Albany,'' ''Holston,'' and ''Spring Place'' (a popular singing convention center near Knoxville).

A number of early country music stars, including Kirk McGee and the Delmore Brothers, have recalled learning rudiments in the old singing schools. A. P. Carter, founder of the Carter Family, got his early training in church quartet music about the turn of the century. It was the all-day singings and singing schools that eventually paved the way for gospel music, modern-day country music's religious counterpart. In fact, religious music was commercialized and adapted to modern mass media as fast or faster than traditional secular music; and, as noted in chapter 2, Tennessee became a center for commercialized gospel music far sooner than it did for commercialized secular music.

Though most of the old ballad singers and church singers in the Tennessee mountains sang unaccompanied, there was from the earliest days in Tennessee a healthy instrumental tradition centering around the fiddle. Many of the early settlers in the area brought with them fiddling tunes and traditions from Scotland and Ireland. Many old fiddle tunes, like many old ballads, can be traced back to Old World origins, though it is more difficult to do this with an instrumental tune. Many immigrants took Old World tunes and simply gave them Americanized names, sometimes with surrealistic results: ''Bonaparte's Retreat'' was known in some areas as ''Bonaparte's Retreat Across the Rocky Mountains,'' and the old jig ''Soldier's Joy'' became known in some quarters as ''Soap Suds Over the Fence.'' ''Miss McLeod's Reel'' was rechristened ''Did You Ever See a Devil Uncle Joe.'' Still other rural fiddlers took strains from one tune, combined them with phrases from another, and added some original passages, creating totally new tunes. They dubbed them with colorful names; some tunes common in East Tennessee in the 1870s included "Old Granny Rattletrap," "Chicken in the Bread-Pan Scratching Out Dough," "Jenny Put the Kettle On," "Sail Away Ladies," "Shoot Old Davy Dugger," "Turkey Buzzard," and the most famous pieces, "Arkansas Traveller" and "Turkey in the Straw" (probably based on an old English tune, "The Jolly Miller").

Fiddle music was basically social music, used for rural dances or "hops" or "frolics." Often at these dances the fiddler alone would provide the music; at a dance in the nineteenth century there were virtually no guitarists and few banjoists to back up a fiddler at a dance. Many old-time fiddlers, having to carry a melody and generate a danceable rhythm at the same time, devised complex and exciting solo styles for their tunes. We have no idea of how many of the early nineteenth-century folk styles sounded; no one wrote them down, and there were obviously no phonograph records or tape recorders. But we do have phonograph records made in the early 1920s by old fiddlers who learned their styles as early as the 1860s, and these records suggest that the older solo styles were rather slow (at least by modern bluegrass standards) and full of careful, deliberate rhythms. One musicologist recently tried to analyze a three-minute recorded solo by Uncle Bunt Stephens, an old solo fiddler from Moore County, Tennessee, and had to take some twenty-six pages in a scholarly journal to describe and analyze the piece adequately.

Not only was the music of old-time solo fiddling quite different from much of the fiddling we hear today, but the actual manner of playing the fiddle was quite different. Most fiddlers today place their instrument under the chin, hold it steady, and manipulate the bow with the wrist. Old-timers scoff at this; "That's the way you play a violin," said one; "a fiddle's played on the arm." Mountain fiddlers often held their instrument down off their shoulder in the crook of their arm, and they usually moved their instrument as much as their bow. Other nineteenth-century accounts describe fiddlers holding the body of the fiddle against the breast. Fiddlers in the eastern half of the state also used a short, or "jiggy," bow in their playing; this made their music rather choppy and full of short, highly rhythmic passages. By the 1920s many old fiddlers were playing the "long bow" or "Texas" style, which depended more on complex fingering and yielded smooth, long passages, and the short bow style was on its way out. But the short bow style often made up in excitement and drive what it lost in technical finesse, and it certainly fulfilled its purpose. It was dance music, not especially listening music (as so much "long bow" music of today is), and like ballad singing, the short bow style is in danger of extinction today.

Fiddlers were not known as singers, but they would frequently relieve the monotony of long dances by singing little "jig" couplets to their dance tunes. Many of these couplets were simple, funny, and interchangeable with a number of different tunes.

If you can't get the stopper out, break off the neck,
If you can't get the stopper out, break off the neck,
If you can't get the stopper out, break off the neck,
And we'll go marching on.

Others were slightly off-color and even more down to earth:

Sally will your dog bite, No sir no,
Daddy cut his biter off a long time ago,
Sally in the garden sifting sand,
Sally upstairs with a hog-eyed man.

"Hog-eyed" probably means "wall-eyed," but no one is sure, and the context here seems clear enough. It is, incidentally, very difficult to sing and fiddle at the same time, and few fiddlers today can do it; but the combination was apparently rather common in the nineteenth and early twentieth centuries in rural Tennessee.

The fiddler's role in the community was not quite like that of the ballad singer. Many of the strict pioneer religions frowned on the fiddle or on instrumental music of any sort; the fiddle became known in some communities as "the devil's box," and stories were told of people finding old fiddles walled up within old cabins, put there when their owners "got religion" and stopped fiddling, yet could not bring themselves to destroy their beloved instruments. The common expression "as thick as fiddlers in hell" ("so thick they couldn't move their bows back and forth") reflects an all-too-common reaction of southern Protestants toward fiddling; fiddling was equated with laziness, and laziness with sin. Hence the modern expression, "fiddling around." Yet in other communities fiddles were brought openly into church, and we have a few recorded instances of string bands being used to play for revival meetings.

But most fiddlers played for dances. Such fiddlers were much in demand on the frontier; A. W. Putnam, in his *History of Middle Tennessee*, published in Nashville in 1859, describes a famous Tennessee fiddler of the 1790s, James

Rural fiddlers such as these anonymous musicians from Middle Tennessee often gave new names to Old World tunes or added original passages to combinations of the old to create entirely new selections. Note position of the fiddle and that the banjoist has removed some of his banjo's frets.

Gamble. Gamble, carrying his fiddle in "a sack of doeskin," was popular
throughout Middle Tennessee, from Sumner County to "the Bluff" (Nashville). Putnam writes: "Whenever there was to be much of an entertainment
or considerable dance, the girls would say, 'O, get Gamble! Do get Gamble!
We know he will come.' And Gamble was indeed always willing to come.
This was his pleasure; he had no other business, he did nothing else. . . ."
When the Great Revival came to the area in the early 1800s, many fiddlers of
the region gave up fiddling, but Gamble did not. "He read his Bible, and
fiddled; he prayed, and he fiddled; asked a silent blessing on his meals, gave
thanks, and fiddled; went to meetings, sang the songs of Zion, joined in all the
devotional services, went home, and fiddled. He sometimes fiddled in bed,
but always fiddled when he got up." In fact, a popular story of the area tells of
Gamble escaping an Indian attack, receiving several arrow wounds, and
spending several weeks in bed recovering and inventing a piece on his fiddle
that imitated the attack, the Indian screaming, and his escape. Gamble, "the
most distinguished fiddler in all the district of Mero," was well known in the
territory ten years before Tennessee became a state in 1796.

Apparently a great many rural Tennesseans in the nineteenth century could
fiddle some, though few had a repertoire of more than a dozen or so tunes. A
fiddler who could play for longer periods of time was usually sought for
dances, and widely admired in the community; when most people bragged
about their community fiddler, they usually bragged about the large number of
tunes he played, not especially about his technical skill or inventiveness. The
fiddler was usually paid in free food and drink, though in some cases he was
paid in cash. Sam McGee, veteran Grand Ole Opry star, described such a
dance that he remembered playing at in Middle Tennessee about 1910:

> They always held them in someone's home. . . . They'd just dance on
> whatever kind of floor it was. When they got ready to dance, they'd dance.
> I've seen 'em put sawdust and meal down on the floor to dance on—it made
> the feet easy to slide. We'd have to play on these dances probably all night
> long . . . until just about day or maybe even day. We were paid—three
> figures would be called a set and they'd charge them, have a man go around
> and take up money from all of them, 10¢ a set. Well . . . these callers
> would call a set so long; maybe they'd dance twenty minutes on one figure,
> and it would take three of them. We'd play one tune for twenty minutes
> without stopping. . . . They'd treat you like you were a king. About
> 12 o'clock they'd always have a lot of stuff cooked up and you could go in
> and eat or drink anything you wanted to, and the first thing you know, they
> were lined up and going again. Knocking dust . . . They'd have us up on a
> platform in a corner, and that dust would come up—your eyes would look
> like two burnt holes in a blanket.

As fiddling gained popularity, a separate folklore built up about fiddlers and fiddling. Whenever fiddlers gathered together to compete in a contest or just to visit, talk often turned to fiddles and fiddle lore. There were stories about how different fiddle tunes got their names. "Billy in the Low Ground," for instance, originated with an old fiddler named Billy who fell into a sinkhole and played his fiddle to attract help. "The Eighth of January" originated in commemoration of Tennessean Andrew Jackson's victory in the battle of New Orleans on January 8, 1815 (and in more modern times words have been added and the song made into a popular country hit by Johnny Horton). "Tennessee Waggoner" refers to the driver of an ox-pulled Conestoga wagon, or to a popular adaptation of an air by the German composer Wagner, depending on whom you talk to. There are some fiddle tunes that have the same name as old quilt patterns, such as "Virginia Reel," "Dusty Miller," and "Golden Wedding." There was also a lore of fiddle-making, for many mountaineers made their own fiddles. Materials ranged all the way from cigar boxes to syrup buckets with wooden necks; hair from a mule's tail strung the bow, and pine off a pine tree was rosin for the bow. More serious fiddlers crafted fine instruments from wood; many preferred curly maple for the back and sides and spruce for the top. Old fiddles became prized heirlooms, passed from generation to generation, and a good fiddler invariably included in his lore a history of his fiddle. There were special ways to care for a fiddle: rattlesnake rattles left inside the body improved the tone, and a silk cloth laid across the "breast" of a fiddle helped protect it in its case. Many old-timers even had pet names for their fiddle; Uncle Jimmy Thompson, the first fiddler on the Grand Ole Opry, called his instrument "Old Betsy."

By the last two decades of the nineteenth century, fiddling began to attract a certain amount of attention as a folk art, or at least as a respected skill. Fiddling contests were held across the state in increasing numbers, and fiddlers soon found occasions other than dances to play for. These gatherings gave fiddlers a chance to match their skills, exchange tunes, and have a general good time. At the most basic level, the contests were community affairs, often held in rural schoolhouses or meeting halls. A description of such a turn-of-the-century contest held in the Smoky Mountains was published by folklorist Louise Rand Bascom in 1909:

The convention is essentially an affair of the people, and is usually held in a stuffy little schoolhouse, lighted by one or two evil-smelling lamps, and provided with a rude, temporary stage. On this the fifteen fiddlers and 'follerers of banjo pickin' sit, their coats and hats hung conveniently on pegs above their heads, their faces inscrutable. To all appearances they do not care to whom the prize is awarded, for the winner will undoubtedly treat. Also, they are not bothered by the note-taking of zealous judges, as these gentlemen are not appointed until after each contestant has finished his allotted 'three pieces.'

To one unused to the mountain tunes, the business of selecting the best player would not be unlike telling which snail had eaten the rhododendron leaf, for execution and technique differ little with the individual performers, and the tune, no matter what it may be called, always sounds the same. It is composed of practically two bars which are repeated over and over and over again until the fiddler or banjo picker, as the case may be, stops abruptly from sheer fatigue. . . . The tunes are played at all the dances, whistled and sung by men and boys everywhere. The mountaineer who cannot draw music from the violin, the banjo, or the 'French harp' is probably non-existent. . . . The women are also endowed with musical talent; but they regard it as the men's prerogative, and rarely touch an instrument when their husbands or sons are present.

By the turn of the century the banjo had made its way into the mountains, but few accounts describe the playing of the banjo and fiddle together; the fiddle was still the main instrument, though the French harp, or harmonica, as well as the banjo, was a common instrument. The fact that mountain women—even those with musical talent—were reluctant even to touch the instruments in their men's presence is suggestive of a curious relationship between sexual gender and folk music. We have very few instances of mountain women making instrumental music, but when we turn to vocal music—ballad singing—women were the singers more often than men. In Professor Boswell's collection of over 770 Tennessee folk songs, over 66 percent of his informants were women. In a very general sense, we might say that the typical rural nineteenth-century community saw vocal music as women's prerogative, fiddling as men's prerogative; perhaps ballad singing was seen as a form of culture, whereas fiddling was seen more as a physical skill.

Contests on a larger scale were held at county seats, ususally in the courthouse and during the sessions of the quarterly circuit courts. Often the highest praise a fiddler could receive was "best in the county," for in an age of poor roads and rough hilly country, the width of a county often meant a hard

The prominence of these Market House fiddlers (top), performing in Knoxville about 1886, attests to the popularity of early fiddling contests in the state. From left, they are Dr. Dave DeArmond, Governor Bob Taylor, Shed Armstrong, and Bartley Griffin. The anonymous string band (bottom), photographed about 1900, includes a cello, which was not uncommon in early days.

day's journey. These contests were usually officiated by "judges" of some sort, sometimes simply members of the audience who enjoyed fiddling, at other times prominent members of the community, and on occasion other (and sometimes older) fiddlers who for various reasons would not or could not compete. The criteria used in judging these nineteenth-century contests varied from community to community, and exactly what, in the way of technique, constituted "good fiddling" for many of these contests is not at all clear.

Even larger towns often staged fiddling contests as part of their holiday celebrations. In Morristown, for instance, local fiddling contests were often held as part of the Fourth of July celebration. In the late 1880s and early 1890s, Knoxville held contests as part of the Labor Day celebrations. An account from the Knoxville *Tribune* of August 30, 1891, lists the fiddling contest as part of the "Amusement Program," which included a mule race, a tug of war, a typesetting contest, and "toddy tail-pulling." (The fiddling prize was $3.00, compared to a $10.00 prize for typesetting.) People certainly did not pay the close attention to the fiddlers that they do at a modern contest, when fiddling almost seems elevated to the status of a high art. And the music for the dances of this particular outing was not even provided by fiddlers, but by a brass band. One aspect of this nineteenth-century contest, though, was to be a part of nearly every fiddling contest since, including those of today: nostalgia. Even in 1891 people were seeing fiddling as a link to the "good old days"; the Knoxville *Tribune* commented that the fiddling contestants "might have been called to bewitch the soul of that merry monarch of song, Jolly old King Cole, and each played the sweet old tunes of by gone time with charmed bow string." Even Louise Rand Bascom's 1909 account stresses the fact that "the tunes are very old. One fiddler, aged ninety-four, states that he is playing his great-grandfather's 'pieces.' " In a very real sense, fiddling has always been a product of genuine folk tradition, often passed on from generation to generation, and is thus an affirmation of heritage; but even in the popular mind, fiddling has, more than any other folk music, been associated with grass-roots American values. These earliest documented contests in Tennessee reveal this same popular attitude.

Tennesseans affirmed this attitude even more strongly in their response to the famous "fiddling governor," Bob Taylor. Robert Love Taylor (1850–1912) was governor of Tennessee from 1887 to 1891 and again from 1897 to 1899; he was also a United States congressman and a United States senator during his long public career. Taylor was an extremely popular figure in Tennessee politics; he projected an image of a down-to-earth country boy, and this image was fostered in part by Taylor's love of old-time fiddling.

Bob Taylor in fact had genuine rural roots, hailing from remote Carter

County in the northeast corner of the state. When Taylor was only ten, in 1860, he was enchanted by two local fiddlers playing at an old log schoolhouse. Bob soon learned to fiddle, as did his older brothers Alf and Jim, and often all three Taylor brothers would perform at school "exhibitions," Bob usually playing second fiddle, or alto, to one of his brothers. Bob was soon playing tunes like "Tramp the Devil's Eyes Out," "Jennie, Blow the Fire Strong," "Hole in the Kettle," "Turkey Buzzard," and "Sally Ann." Bob's brothers were later to recall: "According to the ideas of *us* mountaineers, fast and lively music is the only music. The fellow that can play the fiddle like an empty thresher under a full head of steam is considered the only fiddler worth listening to."

Although Bob Taylor played the fiddle only as a hobby, he soon found that it had certain political advantages: it helped his image as a rural "man of the people." As Taylor's fame spread, the popular press was quick to seize on his fiddling as a colorful characteristic. In Taylor's first election in 1878, his opponent circulated a piece of doggerel declaring "Bobbie Taylor, he / Is the biggest fiddler in Tennessee"; congressmen would "rather hear Bob's fiddle squeak / Than to hear the ablest statesman speak." In 1886 Bob campaigned for governor against his own brother Alf in the famous "War of the Roses"; the popular press, especially in the North, sensed the drama and romance of this brother-against-brother race and further emphasized the role fiddling played in the race. A picture of the two brothers fiddling against each other on the campaign platform was widely circulated, although modern research has failed to document many instances of Bob actually fiddling on the campaign platform. An 1890 account by Murfreesboro writer Wil Allen Dromgoole pictures Bob Taylor as "fiddling his way to fame" and shows him in one scene pacifying angry constituents not by logic or rhetoric but by simply fiddling a favorite sentimental tune.

Thus the fiddler image both helped and hindered Taylor. Enemies accused him of evading difficult campaign issues by pulling out his fiddle; many Tennesseans still saw the fiddle as "the devil's box" and associated it with laziness or frivolity. This is probably why, after Taylor died in 1912, his family sought to minimize his fiddling abilities and to call attention to his genuine and considerable political achievements. Yet there is no doubt that Taylor did love fiddling and even entered fiddling contests while holding the governor's office. He himself wrote of his first campaign: "Unable to bear the armour of a Saul, I went forth to do battle armed with a fiddle, a pair of saddlebags, a plug horse, and the eternal truth." In an 1899 public letter addressed "To the Fiddlers," Taylor made a passionate and eloquent defense of his fiddling, and fiddling in general: "Politicians sneered at me as a fiddler;

FRANK LESLIE'S
ILLUSTRATED
NEWSPAPER

No. 1,619.—Vol. LXIII.]   NEW YORK—FOR THE WEEK ENDING OCTOBER 2, 1886.   [Price, 10 Cents.

ALFRED A. TAYLOR.   ROBERT L. TAYLOR.

NOVEL POLITICAL CAMPAIGN IN TENNESSEE—THE RIVAL CANDIDATES, "ALF" TAYLOR AND "BOB" TAYLOR, FIDDLING FOR VOTES.

FROM A SKETCH BY GEORGE SIMONS.—SEE PAGE 101.

but the girls said it was no harm, and the boys voted while I fiddled, and the fiddle won. . . . "Happy is the home in which fiddles and fiddlers dwell, and nearest to heaven is the church where fiddlers and singers blend their music in hymns of praise to Almighty God.''

When he was not in office, Taylor enjoyed tremendous success as a lecturer, and his most famous lecture was ''The Fiddle and the Bow.'' In this presentation, which Taylor gave all over the state, he used the fiddle as the central image around which he grouped a long series of rural, sentimental, nostalgic scenes. In fact, these scenes, which Taylor wrote at the end of the nineteenth century, could easily represent the various aspects of folk music in nineteenth-century Tennessee. He describes a rural school exhibition, where country fiddlers sat on stage playing ''Old Dan Tucker'' in unison and where fiddling alternated with ''dramatic orations'' and readings of ''compositions'' by students. He also describes a quilting bee and a dance which follows it. The sets are called by Old Uncle Ephraim, a black man ''attired in his master's old claw-hammer coat, a very buff vest; a high standing collar, the corners of which stood out six inches from his face; striped pantaloons that fitted as tightly as a kid glove, and he wore number 14 shoes.'' Taylor also describes scenes at a formal banquet featuring the more popular and light classical music of the day and a scene at an old singing school. Regardless of whether he used the fiddle to enhance his political image or to appeal to lecture crowds hungering for nostalgia, Governor Bob Taylor was remarkably perceptive about the nature and scope of Tennessee folk music. He honestly enjoyed fiddling and was smart enough to see it complemented his own brand of politics. And in this association of fiddling with a particular political image, Governor Bob was blazing the trail for future politicians as diverse in political philosophy as Alf Taylor (in the 1920s), Grand Ole Opry star Roy Acuff (in the 1940s), and Senator Albert Gore (in the 1960s). All of these men were to bring fiddling into Tennessee politics.

During one of his terms as governor, probably in 1890, Bob Taylor attended a rural barbecue and rally at Copperhill, Tennessee. While there he watched a tall rawboned lad fresh out of the nearby north Georgia hills play the fiddle. The Governor was so impressed that he asked the boy's name. ''John Carson,'' was the response. ''Well, from now on it's Fiddlin' John Carson,'' said the governor, and he bought the boy his first store-bought

This New York newspaper of 1886 illustrates the nationwide attention given to the Taylor brothers' ''War of the Roses,'' in which Bob and Alf campaigned against each other for governor. Both were fiddlers, and the popular press was quick to capitalize on the human interest of this hobby.

clothes and his first good fiddle. The young man soon became good friends with the governor and apparently helped him campaign some. Once the governor took on the young man in a fiddling contest in Memphis; the two fiddlers tied again and again. Finally the judges awarded the prize to Governor Bob. The governor, however, refused the prize and gave it to John Carson, proclaiming him the South's finest fiddler. Carson was barely in his twenties at the time, and though Governor Taylor never was to know it, Fiddlin' John was, in a few short years, to revolutionize the role of old-time fiddling in American life and to become the first country music recording star.

2. Out of the Hills:
The First Professionals

Fiddling and banjo picking were thriving in the mountains of Tennessee and Cecil Sharp had published his collection of mountain songs, but most Americans at the beginning of the 1920s were not aware of a genre of music called "country." Although new forms of mass media—records and radio—were beginning to make their impact across America, these media had not yet appreciated hill country music. By 1920 the record industry was booming, but its products were aimed at the affluent upper and middle class: people who preferred light opera, parlor songs, dance orchestras like Waring's Pennsylvanians and Paul Whiteman and Zez Confrey. Rural Tennesseans, like most rural southerners, were aware of Victrolas and records, but they saw little in Victrola music to interest them.

All this was to change within a few years. More and more radio stations started up around the country. The awkward crystal sets (on which only one person could listen at a time) gave way to radio speakers, which brought sound into the whole room. "The miracle of radio" caused sales of records to plummet disastrously; Victor sales, for instance, fell by over half between 1921 and 1925. Why should a person pay to hear music on records when he could hear it free over the airwaves? So the record companies, in order to survive, had to look more closely for new markets. One of the new markets was the "hillbilly" market. In June 1923 the Okeh Record Company had recorded, as a favor to a local client, an old Atlanta fiddler named Fiddlin' John Carson. Carson was the same fiddler who had played with Governor Bob Taylor, and he came from Fannin County, Georgia, just across the Tennessee state line. He recorded two songs: an old minstrel show number called "The Little Old Log Cabin in the Lane" and an old fiddle tune, "The Old Hen Cackled and the Rooster's Going to Crow." Although northern recording executives thought the record sounded "pluperfect awful," they released it as a favor to their client. Within a matter of weeks, the record was selling into the thousands; today it is recognized as the first country record. It made John Carson the first country recording star, but more important, it showed the record companies that there was a market in the South for traditional, old-time music. And with the record industry in a severe slump, the hillbilly market was one that became more and more appealing.

By 1924 the different record companies began to record southern music. The Columbia and Okeh companies, the first into the field, concentrated on recording talent from Georgia and North Carolina; but by mid-1924 the Aeolian-Vocalion Company had discovered Tennessee artists, and they had brought to New York the men who were to become Tennessee's first country music recording stars: champion fiddler Uncle Am Stuart, singers Charlie Oaks and George Reneau, and the irrepressible banjoist and singer, Uncle Dave Macon.

Uncle Am Stuart was a product of the carefree nineteenth-century fiddling traditions of the mountains of East Tennessee. He was born in 1856 or 1857 in Morristown, near the area where the Taylor brothers lived, and he apparently learned his fiddling style and many of his tunes shortly after the Civil War. His recordings made in 1924—late in his life—represent probably the oldest fiddling styles preserved on wax, and they made him the country's most popular old-time fiddler after John Carson. Not that Uncle Am thought much about it; his reputation in Morristown was that of a clever safe salesman, an organizer of local fiddling "entertainments," and a generous humanitarian ("If anyone in town ever needed coal in the winter, Uncle Am would see to it that they got it," recalls one neighbor.).

When Uncle Am went to New York in June 1924, he made quite a hit. Between recording sessions, he broadcast over station WJY near Times Square—probably the first mountain fiddler to be heard over radio in the Northeast. A well-known radio reviewer of the day wrote that "Uncle Am's playing made me feel reckless the rest of the evening." Uncle Am's picture appeared in New York newspapers, with the *Herald-Tribune* describing him as "champion of the old time puncheon floor fiddlers of the south" and reporting that he "smokes cigarettes, drinks corn likker and likes the girls." Uncle Am played old southern tunes he had heard, he said, at southern dances "befo' th' wah." In fact, Uncle Am gave the papers quite an account of his life:

> "Ah just nach'ly had to fiddle," Uncle Am explains. "Ever since Ah was big enough to hold a fiddle Ah've been fiddlin'. Ah used to fiddle

In September 1925 radio came to Nashville, and the Banner *ran ads like this to promote "the miracle of radio." The awkward crystal set with its audience-limiting earphones soon gave way to speakers that brought sound to an entire room.*

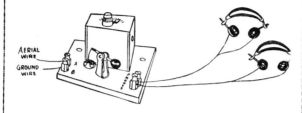

around th' kitchen till mah mother she'd chase me out of theah; and Ah's go down and fiddle aroun' th' niggah camps till they'd chase me out of theah. Then Ah's go into th' barn all alone and fiddle theah. Ah guess Ah learned most of my fiddlin' in that ol' barn.

"Why, man, Ah guess if Ah should go out into th' woods an' go down on my knees to git religion in th' spirit of determination Ah went about my fiddlin', why, Ah wouldn't be surprised if Ah should just nach'ly get religion."

Uncle Am also insisted, every time his picture was printed in the New York papers, that it be "plainly stated" that he was from Morristown, Tennessee.

The company released fourteen selections by Uncle Am, including early versions of fiddle standards like "Waggoner," "Grey Eagle," "Cumberland Gap," "Leather Breeches," and "Sourwood Mountain." (It is a tribute to the endurance of these old fiddle tunes—which Uncle Am probably learned in Civil War days—that they are still very often played at Tennessee fiddling contests and on the Grand Ole Opry.) Am's records were so popular that the company advertised them all over the country in an early attempt to increase the appeal of southern music. Certainly people across the South listened; one young man who listened with special attention was a young boy in Fountain City named Roy Acuff. But Uncle Am did not live to enjoy much of this newly found fame; he died the next year, in 1925.

The vocal traditions of the mountains of East Tennessee were carried into the recording studio by Charlie Oaks and George Reneau. Oaks, as noted earlier, was a veteran minstrel who had been active for some years in the Knoxville area. Although he might have been a native of Kentucky, he spent much of his time in Tennessee, and his songs often reflected this background. By 1924 Oaks was performing his songs with a guitar and a harmonica held around his neck on a holder, forming a sort of one-man band and anticipating a technique to be used by generations of later folk singers, from Woody Guthrie to Bob Dylan. Oaks continued to specialize in topical "event" songs. His early offerings included "The Death of William Jennings Bryan," "The John T. Scopes Trial" (both about the famous 1925 "monkey trial" in Dayton, Tennessee) and a version of Andrew Jenkins' popular "The Death of Floyd Collins." Yet he also recorded older topical songs, including a couple of World War I patriotic songs and a song about "Little Mary Phagan" who

Fiddlin' John Carson (left), first of the country recording stars, poses at a 1926 fiddling contest with another early star, the colorful Uncle Am Stuart, Tennessee champion fiddler. Their performances helped convince the record companies that "Southern" music was a highly marketable item.

had been murdered some twelve years before; this suggests that some topical songs remained popular for years after the events they described. Oaks also sang some sentimental songs and a few delightfully humorous pieces. He was one of the few pre-commercial musicians to make the transition into the new mass media world of phonograph records, but his success was short lived. He apparently never got to broadcast on radio, and his rather archaic performing style was soon outmoded on records by newer and slicker singing styles. He ended his career singing with his wife on Knoxville street corners for nickels and dimes.

A similar fate befell singer George Reneau, "The Blind Minstrel of the Smoky Mountains" (as his record labels described him). He was a young man in his twenties when he was discovered playing his harmonica and guitar on the streets of Knoxville; he was discovered by the Sterchi Brothers Furniture Company, the East Tennessee agents for the Aeolian-Vocalion Record Company, and was sent to New York in May 1924 to record. Reneau's voice, however, was a little too rough (or authentic) for the ears of the recording executives; he had good songs, played the guitar and harp well, but had an untrained voice. The company finally decided to release the records under Reneau's name, have him play instrumental accompaniment, but have most of the singing done by their New York studio singer, Gene Austin. Thus Austin, who was anything but a country vocalist (he went on to become the Bing Crosby of the 1920s), contributed to the recording career of a pioneer country artist, making his recording of the song country music's first million-seller. Reneau later got to record his own singing, and for a couple of years was one of Vocalion's most prolific artists, recording over fifty songs. Many were sentimental songs, but many were also genuine native folk ballads, such as "Wild Bill Jones," "Wild and Reckless Hobo," and "Rovin' Gambler." One of his most popular records was "Here, Rattler, Here," later featured by Grandpa Jones. Reneau later recorded for Thomas Edison's company; then Reneau, too, saw his singing technique go out of style. Love songs, yodel songs, and blues made the old solo ballad, or sentimental style, obsolete; and Reneau, like Oaks, drifted off into obscurity after having a fleeting taste of fame.

The fourth pioneer Tennessee recording artist, Uncle Dave Macon (1870–1952), was to have a more successful career. It began with his singing and banjo playing on the vaudeville stage and at rural schoolhouses after World War I and extended to appearances on television in the early 1950s. During this time he became one of the most beloved entertainers in the history of country music. His records are still enjoyed by millions who never saw him perform, and people who know nothing else about his generation of country artists recognize his name. Some of his records made over fifty years ago are still in print. Folklorists have said of Uncle Dave: "With the exception of the Carter Family, Uncle Dave preserved more valuable American folklore through his recordings than any other folk or country music performer." Radio historians refer to him as "the first featured star of the Grand Ole Opry." The popular press of his day referred to him as "the Dixie Dewdrop," or "the King of the Hillbillies." Yet Uncle Dave described himself merely as "banjoist and songster, liking religion and meetings, farming, and thanking God for all His bountiful gifts in this beautiful world He has bestowed upon us."

Like George Reneau and Uncle Am Stuart, Uncle Dave began recording in 1924; but unlike them he continued to record throughout his career. Had he done nothing but record, his fame would have been assured, for during his career he recorded over 175 songs that were vastly popular throughout the South and even into the Midwest. He made the transition from folk musician to professional musician with zest, and as he frailed his banjo, stomped his feet, and crowed out songs like "Keep My Skillet Good and Greasy," "Chewing Gum," "I'll Tickle Nancy," and "You Can't Do Wrong and Get By," audiences throughout the South whooped and shouted their applause. Whether in vaudeville halls, country schoolhouses, tobacco auctions, in front of old-fashioned radio horns, or by Victrola speakers, the people of Tennessee took to their hearts their very first home-grown country music star.

Unlike Reneau, Oaks, and Stuart, who were from the eastern part of the state, Uncle Dave hailed from a hamlet called Smart Station near McMinnville on the Highland Rim. As a teenager, David Harrison Macon (as he was called then) lived in Nashville, where his father, a former Confederate Army officer, operated the old Broadway Hotel. This hotel catered to the many vaudeville and circus performers who came through Nashville in those days, and the young Macon learned to love their songs and music. He also remembered many of the songs he had learned from Negroes around McMinnville as a child, and—as he later admitted—much of their music found its way into his vocal style. Soon Uncle Dave married and moved back to the country—to a farm near Murfreesboro—and there continued to sing and learn old folk songs from people in the community. He formed a freight hauling company, the Macon Midway Mule and Transportation Company, and hauled freight with mule teams; many old-timers in the area yet today can recall Uncle Dave singing as he drove along, or stopping to rest under a shade tree and taking out his banjo.

In 1920 Uncle Dave became a victim of technological unemployment; a truck line started in competition with Macon Midway, and Uncle Dave chose

Among the first record companies to discover Tennessee artists was Aeolian Vocalion. This is how an Uncle Dave Macon record appeared to buyers in 1927, when country music was still commonly merchandised as "Southern."

not to compete. At the age of fifty, he began seriously thinking of a new career—one in music. His first public performance (about 1921) was a charity event in Morrison, Tennessee; Uncle Dave recalled later: "The Methodist church there needed a new door. I gave a show, then passed the hat and collected the money, $17.00." Two years later, when he was playing for a Shriner's benefit in Nashville, a talent scout from the Loew's vaudeville theaters heard him and offered him a contract. Uncle Dave suddenly found himself a stage star, and he played his banjo and told his jokes at Loew's theaters around the country; he was so popular that other theater chains tried to buy his contract. In 1923 he hired a young partner, a skinny Nashville fiddler and singer named Sid Harkreader. A little later he added a "buck dancer" to his cast. By 1924 Uncle Dave's name was famous across the South.

Thus in the summer of 1924 the Sterchi Brothers Furniture Company sent Uncle Dave and Sid to New York to make their first records. (Sterchi Brothers, acting as talent scouts for Vocalion records and as distributors for the records, played an important role in encouraging early Tennessee folk musicians.) Some of Uncle Dave's first records were some of his most famous: "Keep My Skillet Good and Greasy," "Hill Billie Blues," and his imitation of an old-time hunt, "Fox Chase." Uncle Dave also got his first look at the big city of New York, and took it in style. Once he went into a barber shop and ordered "the works"; he was presented a bill for $7.50 and was barely able to conceal a gasp. Finally recovering his poise, he muttered, "I thought it would be ten dollars." Afterwards he wrote in his expense book, "Robbed in barber shop . . . $7.50."

Uncle Dave's records were so successful that he was repeatedly called back into the studio during the 1920s; he recorded in New York several times a year. Many of his songs were genuine folk songs similar to the kind Sharp collected, but others were old vaudeville songs, blues, old popular songs, and old hymns. On many of the records he introduced the songs with a story or a joke and often mentioned his friends and neighbors in Tennessee by name. Uncle Dave somehow wanted to make each record sound more personal, to get across with each song some of his own high spirits and good humor. He wanted each record to be a little miniature performance, just like those he used to give on stage—as though he sensed that the new Victrola was a cold and impersonal machine, and he wanted to humanize it. And he succeeded.

Uncle Dave had a little trouble in getting accustomed to recording studios. Kirk McGee, who was with him on several later sessions, recalls:

> The people doing the recording, they had a time handling Uncle Dave, because he wouldn't stay put. He kept getting closer and closer to the mike. He was an old stage man, a vaudeville man, and he wanted to do it just like he was doing for an audience. And the recording man said, "Uncle Dave, you're not before an audience now. We're putting this on wax. You don't have to sing so loud to be heard." And they had a lot of trouble with Uncle Dave stomping his foot. . . . It was a wood floor, and he'd get to reeling and rocking and stomping and he'd shake the floor and vibrate that record stylus and we couldn't record. So they went and got him this pillow to put his foot on. Well, he didn't like that. He said, "I don't like that, 'cause I can't hear my foot; that'll ruin my rhythm."

At other times the recording men were even less successful in controlling Uncle Dave. Once when a young recording supervisor tried to advise Uncle Dave about how to sing, the old man exploded: "Now, cap, I can sing anyway I want to and still be heard. I've got a lot of get up and go. And I've got a smokehouse full of country hams and all kinds of meat to eat up there in Readyville. I've got plenty of wood hauled up, and I don't have to be bossed around by some New York sharpshooter just to make a few records, 'cause I've done my part on the record making anyway.'' History does not preserve any response from the recording supervisor.

Uncle Dave did not get rich off of his records, even though they were selling well; very few country singers did prosper from their records in the early days. For most of the 1920s, Uncle Dave depended on personal appearance tours for most of his income. In 1925 he found another partner, guitarist Sam McGee of Franklin, Tennessee. (For more on Sam's career, see chapter 3.) Sam recalled that he and Uncle Dave traveled hundreds of miles in an old touring car with side curtains on the windows. When Uncle Dave was not booked on the vaudeville circuit, he booked his own shows through a huge personal correspondence. He was his own agent, booker, and advertising agency. But Uncle Dave felt the best advertising was word of mouth; Sam McGee recalled that when he and Uncle Dave came to a town where they wanted to do a show, Uncle Dave would invariably head for the school. There he would offer to do a free show for the children, and the teachers and principal would nearly always oblige. After the show, Uncle Dave would make sure to mention where he and Sam would perform that night (it was often the same schoolhouse), letting the kids carry the word home to their parents. The grapevine would do the rest, and the evening show was usually well attended—at twenty-five cents a head.

When the Grand Ole Opry started in 1925 (see chapter 3), Uncle Dave was one of the first performers; in fact, for some time he was about the only real professional on the show. One local Tennessee resident recalls that his family had one of the first radios in the community, and when they learned Uncle Dave would be on radio, they kept the news quiet; they were afraid that if the neighbors found out they would ''swarm into our house to hear Uncle Dave and trample us.'' For a time Uncle Dave was indeed the Opry's only really big star, and in 1931 he headlined the first touring company sent out by the Opry—Uncle Dave Macon and His Moonshiners. By the early 1930s, he was a regular fixture on the show, and in 1939 he went to Hollywood to star with Roy Acuff in the film version of ''Grand Ole Opry.'' Uncle Dave also toured with such legendary figures as the Delmore Brothers, Roy Acuff, and bluegrass exponent Bill Monroe. Uncle Dave played regularly on the Opry until

Sam McGee (left), a major influence on folk guitar stylings, and the irrepressible Uncle Dave Macon were one-time touring partners, performing for enthusiastic audiences over a wide area. In this pose about 1928, McGee holds a rare 6-string Gibson banjo-guitar he has just purchased.

Records and radio were making heroes of some old-time musicians by the time of the Mountain City fiddler's convention in 1925, when the school auditorium floor almost collapsed under the crowd. Performers posed here

*include Uncle Am Stuart (standing in the front, second from right), and
behind him Fiddlin' John Carson; also fiddler G. B. Grayson (extreme left,
second row from top) and next to him, singer Tom Ashley.*

just a few months before his death. He became one of the Opry's most cherished links with its folk heritage, and he came to symbolize the spirit of old-time country music.

It is hard to comprehend fully the total impact Uncle Dave Macon made on the development of country music in Tennessee and across the country. Everyone who knew him, or just saw him perform, has his favorite story about Uncle Dave; even today, in the new modern Opry house, old-timers spend hours exchanging "Uncle Dave" stories. A collection of them could fill a book: stories of his jokes, his stubborn individuality, his forceful assertion of the value of old-time music, his charity, his temper, his faith; stories of how he once said of Bing Crosby: "He's a nice boy, but he'll never get anywhere until he learns to sing louder, so people can hear"; stories of how he once put down bluegrass banjo king Earl Scruggs by saying, "He ain't a bit funny"; stories of how he would sing a gamey song one minute and a sacred song the next; stories of how he would "go to his grip" for a bottle of Jack Daniels at night and play the organ in church the next morning. In many ways his beliefs and values were those of many country singers who were to follow him; and if people call yodeling Jimmie Rodgers "the father of country music," then Uncle Dave must certainly be "the grandfather of country music." More than anyone else, Uncle Dave took the nineteenth-century folk music and turned it into twentieth-century country music.

But, of course, nobody knew all this in the 1920s. To the people of that time—especially the promoters and record company men—Uncle Dave was just one more example of how popular this old-time music was. The music was becoming even more popular as a result of its exposure through the new media of phonograph records and radio. These new media were reaching back into even the remotest hamlets of the mountains and making heroes out of some old-time musicians. A dramatic example of the effect records had on the popularity of musicians came in May 1925 at a fiddler's convention in Mountain City, Tennessee, a small town just a few miles from the North Carolina line. Here hundreds of people crowded into the high school auditorium, almost collapsing the floor, in order to see people like Fiddlin' John Carson, the Fiddlin' Powers Family, Uncle Am Stuart, Dedrick Harris, and the original Hill Billies Band—all musicians who had established their reputations in the last year and a half through the new phonograph records. The musicians found that people who bought their records were also willing to pay to see them in person; they began to sense the first hints that the day would come when they could make a living playing their folk music.

Most of the first generation of country stars had been solo acts, from the singing and playing of John Carson to the singing of Uncle Dave Macon and

Charlie Oaks. But by the early 1920s a second mode of country music had developed throughout the South: the string band. During the nineteenth century the main instruments of mountain music had been the fiddle and the banjo, but after the turn of the century the guitar gradually made its way into the South. Many people first heard the guitar played by black musicians; others saw it first in the mail-order catalogs of Sears or Wards; still others saw it popularized by the various guitar and mandolin societies that were active in the North in the early twentieth century. Many others learned of the guitar during the Spanish-American War in the early 1890s, when American soldiers watched Spanish musicians in Cuba play the instrument. The guitar was quickly adopted as vocal accompaniment and then integrated into the instrumental dance music of the fiddle and the banjo. Thus the classic country string band was formed: the fiddle to play the melody lead, the banjo to pick a melodic counterpoint, and the guitar to form a rhythm and bass. This was an instrumental line-up that functioned much as the trumpet, clarinet, and trombone functioned for New Orleans jazz, and the string band was to have as much influence on American culture as the New Orleans music.

The first string band to record came from Grayson and Carroll counties in Virginia: Henry Whitter's Virginia Breakdowners went to New York to record in early 1924. A year later one of Whitter's men, John Rector, joined Al and Joe Hopkins and Tony Alderman in Galax, Virginia, to form yet another band; this band, which a New York recording executive named "The Hill Billies," was to become the first country string band to achieve wide popularity on records and radio. But at first the band emphasized singing and corny vaudeville routines as much as genuine instrumental virtuosity; in fact, they often featured the piano, ukelele, and even the accordion in addition to the fiddle, banjo, and guitar. But in mid-1925 the band was joined by one of the most brilliant old-time Tennessee fiddlers, Charlie Bowman. Bowman, of Fordtown, Tennessee (named for some ancestors of Tennessee Ernie Ford), came from one of the most interesting musical families in East Tennessee; both of his daughters and his brothers were all fine musicians and many later recorded. (His daughters, as the Bowman Sisters, were perhaps the first country music sister duet to record.) Charlie himself was born in 1889 and was in his thirties when he joined the Hill Billies and turned professional. It was his fine fiddling that helped establish the musical reputation of the Hill Billies Band.

Charlie was also responsible for one of the Hill Billies' most significant recordings, "Nine Pound Hammer." This song was to become one of the most popular folk songs and country songs of later years, and its refrain ("Nine pound hammer, just a little too heavy, / Baby for my size, baby, for my size'') was to be sung by thousands of people who knew little of its origin. Bowman had actually learned some of the song from Negro railroad construction gangs in East Tennessee about 1905; he added to it and with the help of Hill Billies leader Al Hopkins arranged it for a recording session in 1927. The song thus moved from oral folk tradition into popular music (via the record) and then back into oral tradition. Such interplay was not uncommon in the early days of records, and Charlie Bowman played an important role in popularizing such folk songs. The Hill Billies toured widely in the mid-1920s, not only in the South but also in the North; they broadcast from both New York and Washington, D.C., and recorded under two different names for two companies. The Hill Billies continued to return to East Tennessee to seek out musicians for their band. They persuaded Uncle Am Stuart to play with them for a time, and on several recordings they used the Roe Brothers from near Bristol. Their steel guitar player was Frank Wilson, who later settled around Knoxville and continued to play with the Bowman Brothers after the Hill Billies broke up. By the time the Hill Billies disbanded in 1932, they had successfully established the string band as a popular facet of country music.

In fact, by 1926 numerous country artists were successfully recording as vocalists, as fiddlers, and as string bands; their success encouraged the large recording companies in New York and Chicago to make even further efforts to commercialize the music. Most of the companies, continuing to see their sales fall because of radio, decided to start a specialized series of recordings designed to be marketed and sold mainly in the South. These records would feature country music as performed by native country artists. Although the success of the Hill Billies encouraged some record company executives to label this new music ''hillbilly'' music, others sensed that this was a ''fighting word'' for many southerners. Most of the early country records were described as ''old-time music'' or ''hill country music''; these phrases were more appealing, and the emphasis of ''old-time'' accurately reflected the nostalgia in the music. (The phrases ''country music'' or ''folk music'' were hardly ever applied to this music before the 1930s.) Besides naming the music, though, the recording companies had to find it. Before this time, most of the artists from the South had gone to New York to record. This practice created certain problems for the companies: how to find genuine southern artists and how to make them feel at ease when they recorded. The answer to this problem lay in technology; before 1925, most recording was done by the acoustic method, which required bulky equipment. But in 1925 Victor invented an electrical recording process; in addition to making much clearer recordings, the electrical method meant fewer pieces of bulky equipment. It was possible to record "in the field" as opposed to studios. Since many of the skilled folk performers who appealed to southern audiences were not to be found in New York or Chicago, and since many did not care to leave their jobs and families to journey to the North to audition or record (often for little pay), the obvious solution was for the record companies to go to them.

Thus the era of field recording began. Every year from 1926 through 1931, various "talent scouts" toured throughout the South looking for new talent; they usually traveled with a portable recording studio which could be set up in a matter of hours, a couple of engineers, and a supply of thick wax discs on which to cut the recordings. Sometimes the scouts would work with local record dealers, who would act as advance men, auditioning talent and lining up people to record. At other times, the talent scouts would pull into a town, rent a vacant building, set up shop, and advertise tryouts in the local paper. In still other cases, the companies would cooperate with local radio stations, at times even using their studios to set up recording equipment. The performers who recorded were paid a flat fee, usually $25 to $50 a side, with no prospect of royalties. If the record sold well, the performers might be asked to record again. Many of the musicians recorded only one time, perhaps preserving four or six songs, then faded quickly into obscurity; most were strictly amateur musicians for whom making music—and recording—was little more than an amusing hobby. In the early 1930s the Library of Congress began to send folklorists around the country to preserve on record examples of vanishing folk music; but, in the South at least, the commercial record companies had been doing the same thing ten years earlier, though for less noble reasons. The commercial companies recorded in as many as fifteen southern and midwestern states before 1935.

During the peak period of these recordings (the Depression curtailed them considerably), Atlanta was the town most frequently visited. In fact, most of the genuine country music recorded in the 1920s came from Atlanta: it was the Nashville of the day, and all the major record companies had studios there. But close behind Atlanta in popularity was Memphis, which during the 1920s was the blues center of the country. Blues was as popular with black audiences in the South as old-time music was with white audiences, and Tennessee was a fertile field for both. In fact, on most of the field trips, the engineers recorded black and white artists back-to-back—even though their records were always released in separate series. Four other Tennessee towns besides Memphis hosted field sessions in the 1920s: Bristol, Johnson City, Knoxville, and Nashville. Trips were fairly frequent to the three eastern towns; Nashville, despite its importance as a recording center today, was visited only once by a recording company in the 1920s—by Victor in 1928. Although that session produced the first recordings made in Nashville, it was commercially unsuccessful.

The true dawn of country music was not to occur at Nashville, but at a sleepy little border town some 300 miles to the east. On a hot July day in 1927 a Victor talent scout named Ralph Peer, his wife, and two engineers pulled into Bristol with two cars full of recording equipment. Peer set up a temporary studio about twenty feet from the Tennessee-Virginia line. He told the editor of the local newspaper that he wanted to make records in Bristol because ''in no section of the South have the pre-war melodies and old mountaineer songs been better preserved than in the mountains of east Tennessee and Southwest Virginia.'' Although Peer had a few acts lined up to record, he was really after new talent. But how to attract it? He hit upon the idea of inviting the local newspaper editor to a recording session, which resulted in a series of stories in the newspaper about the project—and the money to be made from it. The ploy worked. The next day Peer was deluged with phone calls, and would-be musicians arrived in Bristol on foot, by car, by train, and even by horse and buggy.

Two of the acts attracted proved to be among the most successful in country music history. The Monday after the story hit, Peer auditioned a local group from nearby Maces Springs, Virginia, who called themselves the Carter Family. Peer let them record ''The Storms Are on the Ocean'' and ''Bury Me Beneath the Weeping Willow'' and invited them back for more sessions; he thereby launched a career that, in various forms, still flourishes today. The Carters, though from Virginia, spent much time in East Tennessee, and their success as vocalists inspired countless hundreds of others. Maybelle Carter's guitar style, in which she played the melodic line in front of an autoharp rhythm back-up, has indirectly influenced almost every country guitar picker; her solo on ''Wildwood Flower'' is one of the most imitated in country music history. And two days after he found the Carters, Peer auditioned a pale young singer from Mississippi who had been playing in Asheville, North Carolina: his name was Jimmie Rodgers. Peer recorded Rodgers' first two songs in Bristol; though neither of them became instant hits, they paved the way for later Rodgers recordings, including his famous ''blue yodels'' and songs like ''T for Texas, T for Tennessee.'' Within a year Rodgers had become the most popular country singer in the nation—actually country music's first real

The wagon driven by Uncle Dave Macon in later life is similar to one he hauled freight in during World War I. The fiddler, Charlie Bowman, played a major role in popularizing folk songs. Ralph Peer (right), an early talent scout, held important recording sessions in Bristol and Memphis.

superstar—and Peer was beating a path back to Bristol to find similar talent. He did not ever again find anyone of the star caliber of the Carters or Rodgers, though he did record some excellent music. And the fantastic success of Rodgers and the Carters helped Peer launch the Peer-Southern publishing company, one of the largest in the world today.

During the first period of the commercialization of country music, every section of Tennessee saw certain of its musicians emerge as local "stars" on record and, later, on radio. Few of them attained the national status of Uncle Dave Macon, the Carter Family, or Jimmie Rodgers, but many of them saw their music spread across the South and even overseas via their phonograph records. Because the recording activity was centered in Atlanta, more Georgia artists got to record than did artists from other states; had Nashville in the 1920s been the recording center it is today, doubtless even more Tennessee performers would have recorded in the 1920s. But the number of natives who did record, and the material they recorded, testifies to the rich variety of musical styles found in the state. A quick tour around the state supports this notion and allows us to chronicle some of the forgotten pioneers of Tennessee country music.

In East Tennessee, in the Johnson City-Bristol area, fiddling and string band music dominated the scene in the 1920s. Many of the artists in the mountainous area knew each other and worked with each other in a variety of bands; there was also considerable interchange with musicians from nearby southwest Virginia and western North Carolina; some of the best-known bands were composed of musicians from different states. One of the most popular Tennessee bands was headed by the Grant brothers, Jack and Claude; this band, which had originally been the backup band for Jimmie Rodgers before his recording audition, called itself the Tenneva Ramblers in deference to the Tennessee-Virginia border which ran through its home base of Bristol. The band recorded several times and did important early recordings of "The Longest Train I Ever Saw" and "Cocaine Blues" ("Take a Whiff on Me"). The area was rich in good mountain fiddlers; one of the most famous was Fiddlin' Dudley Vance, from Bluff City. Vance came from a family of mountain musicians, and had won championship contests in Tennessee, Oklahoma, and Florida; though he recorded only a few times, he was widely known throughout the Southeast. He later operated a country music park and resort in East Tennessee before he died in 1962. Another famous area fiddler and singer was Mountain City native G. B. Grayson. Grayson, who was blind, traveled extensively and recorded often, and is today considered one of the most influential fiddlers of the 1920s. With his partner Henry Whitter, he recorded the original versions of many songs which became widely popular during the folk revival of the 1960s: "Tom Dooley," "Handsome Molly," "Little Maggie (with the Shot Glass in Her Hand)," and fiddle specialties like "Train 45" and "Lee Highway," both of which are still played frequently at bluegrass and fiddling festivals today. Grayson's career was cut short by his tragic death in an automobile accident in 1929.

One of Grayson's early partners was Bristol native Clarence Tom Ashley (1895–1967), a man destined to become perhaps the most famous singer from the area. Ashley spent his early years touring with the medicine shows that frequented the area—a common apprenticeship for would-be entertainers in the days before records or radio—and then roamed around the region doing what he called "busting": playing on street corners, at carnivals, in coalfields on paydays for the miners. He recorded in the mid-1920s with string bands like Byrd Moore's Hot Shots (from Virginia) and the Carolina Tar Heels (from North Carolina), but it was not until 1929 that he was able to make the solo records that were to win him fame. Using only his banjo as accompaniment, he recorded some of the old ballads he had known since childhood: "The Coo Coo Bird" and "The House Carpenter." These were among the oldest songs he knew, and he called them "lassy-makin' tunes" because he learned them at molasses-making time back home. He used a weird banjo tuning (DCCdG) he called "sawmill tuning" to play "The Coo Coo Bird," and the effect sounded like a cross between oriental and blues music. But the Great Depression hit shortly after Ashley recorded, and he never pursued a career as a "single." He had to support his family, and he worked at a number of odd jobs (including, for a time, a stint as black-faced comedian for bluegrass pioneer Charlie Monroe) before he was "rediscovered" for the folk revival movement in the 1960s. As an older man, Ashley was once again performing, often before college audiences in both the North and the South, and played for a time with a band that included guitarist Doc Watson, Clint Howard, and Fred Price.

If the Johnson City-Bristol area music had affinities with Virginia and North Carolina, the Knoxville area had musical ties with both Georgia and Kentucky. A number of north Georgia musicians often traveled to fiddling contests and dances in the Knoxville area, and many Kentucky musicians were attracted to Knoxville as the largest nearby city. The factories in and around Knoxville also attracted people from the nearby hills and provided steady employment for many amateur musicians; other sources of folk music were the coal mines in the hills north of the city. As noted in chapter 1, Knoxville had always been a center for fiddling contests as well as "old harp" singing schools. In the 1920s a number of local businessmen helped foster the commercialization of old-time music. The Sterchi Brothers Furniture Company helped distribute the first records by Tennessee artists and sponsored recording trips by other artists. Frank "Squire" Murphy staged giant fiddling conventions at Market Hall twice a year, conventions which helped popularize the idea of fiddling associations equally with old-time music.

That Knoxville was the home of pioneer singers like George Reneau and Charlie Oaks has been mentioned previously; in the later 1920s other singers from the area became popular through their records. One was Hugh Ballard Cross, from Oliver Springs, Tennessee; Cross recorded widely in the late 1920s and played with the famous Georgia band, the Skillet Lickers, often singing duets with Riley Puckett, the legendary blind guitarist-singer of the band. Cross was one of the first to record "Wabash Cannonball," a song later to be immortalized by Knoxville-area singer Roy Acuff. Cross had a high, lilting tenor voice and liked to sing old sentimental songs; his love for such sentimental or "heart" songs anticipated the later direction country music was to take, away from the old ballads toward the love songs. Cross went on to have a very successful career on the WLS Barn Dance in Chicago (one of the most successful country radio shows) and later became master of ceremonies of the Boone County Jamboree over WLW, Cincinnati. But even more successful than Cross were two blind musicians who started out working and broadcasting from Knoxville: Lester McFarland and Bob Gardner, known popularly as "Mac and Bob." The two men had met at the Kentucky School for the Blind (which attracted many Tennesseans), where Mac had learned to become a music teacher and Bob a piano tuner. (Bob, like Cross, was from Oliver Springs.) They began playing in school houses and at fairs in the early 1920s and developed a style centered on close-harmony duet singing to the accompaniment of mandolin and guitar. This quiet, sweet style was vastly different from the older, louder mountain singing, and it was well suited to sensitive microphones of the new electrical recording process. From 1927 to 1931 they recorded nearly one hundred songs on the Vocalion and Brunswick labels, many of them old sentimental songs and ballads. They toured on the vaudeville circuits and finally went to the WLS Barn Dance, where they remained one of the most popular old-time acts until their retirement in 1950. Mac and Bob appealed to many people who did not like the more traditional aspects of country music, and their duet singing anticipated a style that was to become the most popular form of country music in the 1930s: that of the Delmore Brothers, the Blue Sky Boys, and the Monroe Brothers.

Probably the most popular string band in Knoxville in the late 1920s was the Tennessee Ramblers. The Ramblers, like many early bands, was a family affair—in this case the family of Fiddlin' Bill Seivers. And like the Hill Billies, the Ramblers achieved much success by combining showmanship (such as trick fiddling and playing the guitar with the feet) with authentic old-time music. Bill Seivers' daughter, Willie, was one of the first women in country music to achieve fame as an instrumentalist; she won national recognition as a champion guitarist and was featured in Gibson guitar catalogs of the time. An equally exciting band—more exciting to fiddling devotees— was a band from west of Knoxville called the Roane County Ramblers. These Ramblers were led by Jimmy McCarroll, a native of the area who incorporated into his fiddling some of the tunes and licks learned from his grandmother, who was part Cherokee. The "Indian pieces" helped give McCarroll's band a distinctive sound that won it a Columbia recording contract and a reputation for hard-driving dance music. The Roane County Ramblers' most famous record was "Southern No. 111," a fiddle specialty in which McCarroll imitated a train that ran from Knoxville to Danville, Kentucky. Both the Roane County Ramblers and the Tennessee Ramblers have continued to exist in various forms into the 1970s. Failing to survive the 1930s were lesser known string bands of the area like Ridgel's Fountain Citians, the Smoky Mountain Ramblers (sponsored on radio by a Knoxville dentist), the Southern Moonlight Entertainers (from Coal Creek), Cal Davenport and His Gang, and groups led by pianist Neb Thacker, singer Andy Patterson, and the McCartt Brothers.

Southwest of Knoxville yet another distinct musical climate was developing in Chattanooga, which because of its location, was even more of a crossroads for different musical styles, attracting not only artists from Tennessee but also musicians from north Georgia, Alabama, and Mississippi. From north Georgia came an emphasis on fiddling technique; from the Mississippi delta and from Alabama came an infusion of Negro blues. Chattanooga itself was the birthplace of the most famous blues singer of the 1920s, Bessie Smith, who was as popular with white audiences as with black. As a result of these influences, Chattanooga provided one of the most eclectic musical climates for early country music.

Two groups really dominated Chattanooga music in the 1920s: Jess Young's Tennessee Band and the vocal duet known as the Allen Brothers. Jess Young's group came out of the Sequatchie Valley, northwest of the city, and was sparked by Young's fiddling and the innovative banjo picking of Homer Davenport. Davenport was picking with an unusual three-finger style as early as 1924, and the style sounds much like that popularized in the 1940s by bluegrass musician Earl Scruggs. Davenport might well have developed bluegrass techniques further had his arm not been crushed in a tragic train accident. The Young band also integrated ragtime music into the traditional string band repertoire, some of which Jess and his nephew Alvin learned from black musicians playing on riverboats in the area. Young's specialties included "Maybelle Rag," "Fiddle Up" (another ragtime tune), and a strange Hawaiian rag entitled "Hy Patitian." This last number was also used by the Allen Brothers, and called "Allen Brothers Rag." Austin and Lee Allen, from Sewanee, Tennessee, sang and played with the rather unusual instrumentation of guitar, kazoo, and tenor (as opposed to five-string) banjo. They specialized in rags and blues; in fact, they became so good at performing blues that many of their record fans thought they were black. One company even released one of the Allens' records in the Negro blues series, an act which infuriated both brothers. The Allens were one of the first groups in the area to try to go professional, and for about ten years they struggled along making a living from touring, recording, and even acting before finally giving it up during the depression. The Allens were wildly popular in the 1920s, especially with a song called "Salty Dog Blues," which they established as a country-bluegrass standard. The Allens also popularized many genuine folk songs, such as "Roll Down the Line," which originated in the 1890s at the Lone Rock coal mines near Sewanee. Some Allen songs commented on topical events of the day: "Jake Walk Blues" reflects the dangers of getting "jake leg" from drinking Jamaica Ginger extract from Prohibition days, and "New Deal Blues" is a tribute to the Roosevelt administration's efforts to curb the Great Depression. Folklore scholars had searched for the Allens for years after they dropped out of the music business in the 1930s and only recently found Lee, the surviving member, living in Lebanon, Tennessee.

Other musicians active in Chattanooga during the dawn of country music included Claude Davis, who helped promote fiddling contests and stage shows in the area and was an excellent musician in his own right; Grover Rann and Harry Ayers, who led a band called "The Lookout Mountaineers," the first country band to broadcast in Chattanooga; and Bob Douglas, a national champion fiddler who has led bands in Chattanooga from 1928 to the present and who discovered later country music greats like the Louvin Brothers. Colorful characters like Sawmill Smith and Tom Cat Payne made fiddling contests more interesting.

Middle Tennessee also supplied its share of early country artists. From

Pictured in 1929, the popular Tennessee Ramblers (top) from Clinton featured Bill Seivers (fiddle) and his children Willie (banjo) and Mack (Hawaiian guitar) and nephew Jerry Taylor. The 1928 Vaughan songbook shown is typical of many produced by the influential publisher of gospel music. Right, Jack Jackson of Lebanon, first country singer to record in Nashville (1928), gained fame as "The Strolling Yodeller" over WSM and WLAC.

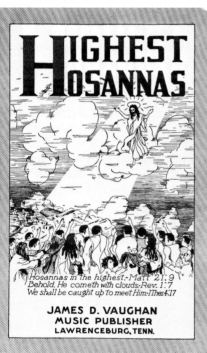

HIGHEST HOSANNAS

Hosannas in the highest.—Matt 21:9
Behold, He cometh with clouds.—Rev. 1:7
We shall be caught up to meet Him.—1 Thes 4:17

JAMES D. VAUGHAN
MUSIC PUBLISHER
LAWRENCEBURG, TENN.

Perry County, on the Tennessee River, came two unique string bands, the Perry County Music Makers, and the Weems String Band. The Perry County Music Makers were built around a zither, a multi-stringed instrument brought into the area by German settlers, and this grouping gave them one of the most distinctive sounds in old-time music. The Perry County Music Makers are still active today and have recently made appearances at folk festivals as far away as Washington, D.C. The Weems String Band often used an archaic fiddle-banjo lead instead of the fiddle-guitar-banjo combination. And from Erin, Tennessee, to the north of Perry County, came ''Ramblin' Red'' Lowery, a Jimmie Rodgers-styled singer and yodeller who specialized in white blues and who later was often heard over Memphis radio.

The West Tennessee area was dominated by the Memphis blues scene, which was nationally recognized as early as the 1920s. The birthplace of W. C. Handy, author of ''St. Louis Blues,'' Memphis was also the home of the Memphis Jug Band, which featured a combination of ragtime, blues, and dance music that influenced white and black music alike. In fact, the first records made in Tennessee were blues records cut in Memphis in 1927. The popular vocal duet of Reece Fleming and Respers Townsend recorded nearly fifty songs in the early 1930s, and their style—especially their duet yodeling—influenced many other duet acts of the 1930s.

But the most popular and influential music in Tennessee was not country music in the strictest sense, but rather the gospel music of the James D. Vaughan Company of Lawrenceburg, Tennessee. Shortly after World War I, James Vaughan founded a singing school in Lawrenceburg and soon branched out into the publication of songbooks, records, and magazines. From the early 1920s to the 1960s, Vaughan was a major force in the development of gospel music throughout the country. He hired quartets to go out and sing his songs to publicize them, and helped promote a whole new type of singing in the South. His singing schools gave generations of southerners their first taste of the ''rudiments'' of music, and many a country singer started out singing gospel songs from one of the 105 songbooks Vaughan published in his career. Vaughan started his own record company in 1922 and used it to promote his own gospel music. In 1924, for the same purpose, he established one of the first radio stations in Tennessee, WOAN. One of his record advertisements claimed that these records were ''the first and only Southern records to be placed on the market,'' and history bears him out. His records were not recorded in the South, but they were the first records designed for a specifically southern audience.

Vaughan's effect was not so much to preserve old folk music, though he did keep alive the old shape-note system of notation. His typical songbook contained an average of 100 songs, and a few of these were old hymns; but most of his songs were newly written gospel songs, songs produced by hundreds of amateur writers across the South. The average songbook sold about 117,000 copies: it was paperbacked, cheap, and easily carried to the singing conventions that dotted the South until the late 1960s. Few of Vaughan's books were actually used in church services, but they were widely used in almost every other church activity.

For many people string bands and ballad singing offered a form of relaxation from the drudgery of farm work or factory work; for others, gospel singing performed the same function. Both groups occasionally commercialized their music—via the record or the gospel songbook—and both returned to their normal lives hardly aware of the impact their semiprofessional music was having on their culture. Melvin Robinette, an older fiddler now living in Tullahoma, Tennessee, shares an attitude typical of many of these early country music performers. When being interviewed about his early days making music, he said, "I thought all that stuff, all that music, was dead long ago. I didn't think anything could ever come of it, or anybody would ever be interested in it. We were just having fun back in those days." Without realizing it, artists such as Robinette created the foundation for country music; their part-time efforts at touring and recording and playing in contests defined a type of music for an entire class of Americans. And in Middle Tennessee, in Nashville, events were taking place that were to illustrate the effect of this music even more dramatically.

3. George Hay and the Grand Ole Opry

On November 9, 1925, George D. Hay arrived in Nashville. Hay's vocation was a relatively new one: he was a radio announcer. Just over two years
before, Hay had been a popular journalist for the Memphis *Commercial
Appeal*, where he wrote a humorous column revolving around dialogue
between a white judge and numerous black defendants. The title of the
column was "Howdy, Judge," and it gave Hay the nickname of "the solemn
old Judge"—even though he was a young man of twenty-eight. When the
Commercial Appeal started radio station WMC in 1923, Hay was "drafted"
and made announcer. He was so successful that within a year he had been
hired by one of the country's most powerful stations, WLS in Chicago. (The
initials stood for "World's Largest Store," and referred to Sears, the station's
owner.) Here Hay had continued his success, announcing his acts in a deep
stylized voice and blowing an imitation steamboat whistle he carried. In those
early days of radio, a powerful station carried easily all over the country, and
Hay was soon known nationally; in fact, later in 1924 he was voted the most
popular announcer in the country. And yet here he was, back in the state he
had started from, back in the South, back in a town a fraction the size of
Chicago. Why?

Nashville's National Life and Accident Insurance Company had decided to
start a radio station. From a relatively modest beginning in 1919, radio had
been growing in popularity in every state; by 1922 510 stations had been set
up, and 89 of them were in the South. Early Tennessee stations included
WOAN in Lawrenceburg (the gospel station operated by James D. Vaughan),
WMC in Memphis, and, a little later, WDOD in Chattanooga and WNOX in
Knoxville. Most of these early stations were owned by a single company,
often a newspaper or a mail-order house, and were first seen as rather
uncertain and novel ways to advertise. In fact, many companies started up
radio stations as a sort of "public service"—until they realized the profit that
could be made from using radio as an advertising medium. Edwin Craig, the

son of one of the founders of National Life, urged the company to experiment with this "miracle of radio" and finally—a bit grudgingly—the company decided to build a station. The projected call letters of the new station, WSM, stood for the company's motto, "We Shield Millions." The fifth floor of the new company building near Capitol Hill in Nashville was made into a studio. Once committed, National Life decided to have the best and the finest station in the country, and they spared no expense. When they hired Hay to come to Nashville, they were not getting him because of his southern background in Memphis or because he had announced for the WLS Barn Dance in Chicago; they were getting him because he was at the time considered the best announcer in the country.

Hay, for his part, was moving a step up: he was not to be merely announcer, but "station manager," with power to develop new shows, new programing ideas. WSM had gone on the air about a month earlier (October 5, 1925) and had settled into a programing routine that pleased the good citizens of Nashville, who proudly referred to their town as "the Athens of the South." The programs included band music, lectures, light classical music, and the dance orchestras of men like Francis Craig and Beasley Smith. Hay noted this, but he also noted that the station could not survive long by appealing only to the limited audience found within the city of Nashville, which had a population of only about 100,000. WSM was broadcasting with 1,000 watts of power, making it one of the two strongest stations in the South and stronger than 85 percent of all other stations in the country. It was going out to a much wider audience than just Nashville, and Hay saw the need to cater to this audience. Much of the audience was rural, and much of it had musical tastes which ran more to the fiddle and banjo than to the violin and cello.

While at Chicago, Hay had announced for WLS's pioneer country music show, the National Barn Dance. He had seen firsthand how successful country music could be on the radio. Starting in 1923, the Barn Dance had become one of the most successful radio shows in the nation. Country music had been broadcast even earlier by southern stations like WSB in Atlanta (starting in 1922) and WBAP in Fort Worth (which initiated the first Barn Dance show in early 1923). In Nashville, a little station called WDAD (or "Dad's," because it was owned by Dad's Radio Supply House), on the air a month before WSM, had broadcast fiddle and string band music with great success, and on at least a couple of occasions Uncle Dave Macon and a string band led by Dr. Humphrey Bate, a rural physician, had appeared on WSM before Hay even arrived in town. So country music was not new to Nashville radio—only the formal recognition of it. Hay began telling people that he was thinking of starting a program in Nashville like the National Barn Dance in Chicago; such a program would be more authentic in Nashville because it could draw on genuine folk performers from the nearby Tennessee hills.

Certainly the time was right. In the fall of 1925 and early 1926 the South was in the midst of an old-time fiddling craze; suddenly everyone wanted to hear old-time fiddlers and recapture America's lost folk arts. Much of this interest had been sparked by Henry Ford, whose success with the Model T had earned him the respect of millions of Americans. Ford saw old-time fiddle music as an antidote to the jazz music and "loose morals" that were sweeping the country; fiddling and square dancing helped keep alive old American values. Ford sponsored a series of fiddling contests at Ford dealerships across the South, and these contests made thousands aware of fiddling. The atmosphere created by Ford's sponsorship helped the cause of country music immensely by making it much more acceptable to radio stations and record companies. And it helped give George Hay the impetus he needed to start a regular old-time-music radio show in Nashville.

The actual start of the Opry is generally thought to be Saturday, November 28, 1925, when Hay asked a white-bearded old fiddler named Uncle Jimmy Thompson to play informally before the WSM microphones. Accompanied by his niece on the piano, Thompson began fiddling. Hay later recalled: "He told us he had a thousand tunes, and offered to answer requests." Phone calls and telegrams began flooding the station, and Uncle Jimmy played for an hour. Hay asked the old gentleman if he were getting tired, and Uncle Jimmy snorted, "Why, shucks, a man don't get warmed up in an hour. I won an eight-*day* fiddling contest down at Dallas, and here's my blue ribbon to prove it." Thompson fiddled on, and Percy Craig carried telegram after telegram into the studio. Hay felt pretty sure that he had his mandate: regardless of what the proper citizens of Nashville felt, the people in the outlying areas wanted old-time music.

Throughout December Uncle Jimmy and his niece held forth on WSM. As we have seen, Uncle Jimmy was not the first one to broadcast old-time music over radio in Nashville. But popular legend has made him the first artist on the show that was to become the Grand Ole Opry, and no wonder: for Uncle Jimmy was the stuff from which legends are made. Born in Smith County twelve years before the Civil War, Uncle Jimmy was playing by the time he was seventeen and might well have learned fiddling from men whose styles

The radio popularity of veteran fiddler Uncle Jimmy Thompson (left) caused George Hay (right) to start a regular "barn dance" on WSM. *Most of the early broadcasts of what was to become the Grand Ole Opry originated in the station's old Studio A (bottom) of the National Life Building.*

and repertoires stretched back to Revolutionary America. He was a farmer, and about the turn of the century he moved to Texas. Here he learned the so-called "long bow" technique, a style distinctively different from southeastern mountain style in that it emphasizes elaborate fancy noting patterns instead of a hard-driving rhythm. He brought this back with him to Tennessee just before World War I. His wife died, and at age sixty-eight Uncle Jimmy decided to remarry. He began to tour around the state, trying to make some money fiddling; he fixed up an old truck, put a little house on back, and had one of the country's first campers. He and his wife, Aunt Ella, would travel around, Uncle Jimmy fiddling and Aunt Ella buck dancing in her long white dress. About 1923 Uncle Jimmy drove his camper all the way back to Texas for a fiddling contest. He told a reporter later: "When I got tired, I'd just drive it in the first open place I found by the road and ask if I could stay all night. 'Yep,' they'd say, and I'd drive it in and fix my bed and git out my fiddle."

Uncle Jimmy wanted to broadcast and record, to "throw my music out across the American," as he would say. But he was a genuine hill man and did not take too kindly to some city ways. His grandson recalls: "The first time he got his engagement on the Opry, Eva, his niece, made him have his pants pressed and cleaned, and he came in there when he got ready to put them pants on, hollered in there and said, 'Hey, thar, who ironed them damn wrinkles in my britches? I like my britches smooth and round—fit my kneecaps. Don't want no crease in 'em!' " Uncle Jimmy also tended to run roughshod over some other early rules of radio, such as time limits. A neighbor recalls, "I remember one night when we called down there and told George Hay to get Jimmy to play 'When You and I Were Young Maggie.' He cut loose on it and he never *did* quit; finally they had to stop him and get him out of the way."

Uncle Jimmy's colorful life, stubborn individuality, and eccentric habits made him the darling of the newspapers, and by the end of 1925 hardly a week passed without some story about him. Henry Ford's champion fiddler Mellie Dunham challenged Uncle Jimmy to a contest and Uncle Jimmy replied, "I'll lay with him like a bulldog." That contest never came off, but Uncle Jimmy was soon swept up in the fiddling craze inspired by the series of contests Ford was sponsoring. When he was not playing in contests, Uncle Jimmy was back in Nashville, broadcasting for as much as an hour at a time. Though Uncle Jimmy may not have known a thousand tunes, that he could broadcast for a solid hour proves he knew many; a list later made up by his niece shows that he played numerous old popular songs from the 1890s and even the 1920s, in addition to old fiddle breakdowns like the "fine quadrille," "Lynchburg," which he recalled learning "on the 4th day of August, 1866." Uncle Jimmy finally got to record a few songs, and preserved a style which is distinctively fancier than that of most other Tennessee fiddlers; modern Opry stars like Roy Acuff and Howdy Forrester have praised Uncle Jimmy's fiddling records.

Like many other old fiddlers, Uncle Jimmy naturally associated fiddling with having a good time, and this meant that he liked to have a jug of Wilson County "white lightning" to lubricate his arm. This eventually led to trouble between him and George Hay, and it is probably one of the reasons that Uncle Jimmy appeared on the radio less frequently after 1926. By 1928 he was making only a few guest appearances. Of course, Uncle Jimmy was getting older—he was seventy-seven when he first broadcast—and as the show became more and more crowded with other acts, he had less and less time to play. Though he died in 1931, Uncle Jimmy even today is remembered well by the people in the hamlet of Laguardo, where he lived. In 1975 the Tennessee Valley Old Time Fiddlers' Association honored Uncle Jimmy by erecting a monument by his grave.

Witnessing the excitement generated by the broadcasts of Uncle Jimmy and other early country artists from Nashville and knowing that National Life wanted to publicize its new series of insurance policies for rural customers, Hay announced in December of 1925 that the "Barn Dance" would be a regular segment of the WSM Saturday night programming. During the first three months he established a roster of regular acts and soon had about twenty-five people lined up to play regularly, without pay, on Saturday nights; most of these were country bands or singers, though the nostalgic appeal of the "Barn Dance" idea at first also extended to local jazz bands, military bands, saxophone sextets, barbershop quartets, gospel singers (including some from James D. Vaughan's school of music), and popular tenors like Little Jack Little. But the country portion of the show won out in the end, and three popular "stars" soon emerged to dominate the Opry's early years: Uncle Jimmy Thompson, Uncle Dave Macon (see chapter 2), and Dr. Humphrey Bate.

A word is in order about Dr. Bate, since he was for years a mainstay of the show, and always opened the eight o'clock program with "There'll Be a Hot Time in the Old Town Tonight." As mentioned earlier, Dr. Bate and "his friends and neighbors from Castalian Springs" (as newspapers billed him) were actually the first persons to broadcast country music in Nashville. His band, which George Hay dubbed "The Possum Hunters," featured Dr. Bate himself on harmonica, Oscar Stone on fiddle, and Burt Hutcherson (who still plays on the Opry) on guitar. The piano player for the band was then thirteen-year-old Alcyone Bate, who was to have a long career on the Opry and WSM. Alcyone recalls that her father's band was not quite the collection of rustic primitives that publicity sometimes made them out to be. Dr. Bate, a practicing physician who went to Florida each winter to fish, was a graduate of the Vanderbilt Medical School and a veteran of the Spanish-American War. He liked all kinds of music, especially the band of John Phillip Sousa, and often played light classical pieces on the harmonica.

Bate learned many of his old instrumental tunes—which are quite unusual—from an old slave when Bate was a boy shortly after the Civil War. Some blues influence is apparent on the band's recordings (they made only a handful in 1928) like "Goin' Uptown," "Take Your Foot Out of the Mud and Put It in the Sand," and "Old Joe." Dr. Bate had formed his first band before 1900, and it included a cello as well as a banjo and guitar. We can only wonder about how it sounded, but it must have been appealing to the people of Middle Tennessee. By the days of World War I, Dr. Bate had two or three little separate bands, including a special Hawaiian band. His daughter recalls playing at "socials," on steamboat excursions down the Cumberland River, and between shows at local movie houses showing silent films. Dr. Bate's music probably included aspects of nearly every type of southern turn-of-the-century pop and folk music.

Dr. Bate's love of the harmonica as an old-time instrument ties him to a distinct and curious Middle Tennessee musical style. For some reason, the Nashville area was full of good harmonica players and harmonica bands. In addition to Dr. Bate's band, there was the Crook Brothers band, which at first featured two harmonicas playing lead; Deford Bailey, the Opry's first black star and harmonica soloist; Charley Melton, who was called "Charlie the French Harp King"; and many others. At no place in the South was the harmonica as popular as it was in Middle Tennessee in old-time music; of course, the harmonica was a good substitute for a fiddle in a band, and it had fewer of the "sinful" connotations of the fiddle. This harmonica tradition was carried on throughout the history of the Opry by artists such as Jimmy Riddle, Onie Wheeler, and even more recently Charlie McCoy. And Dr. Bate taught many of his songs to Herman Crook, whose band still played on the Opry into the 1970s.

When Dr. Bate died in 1936, George Hay wrote a glowing tribute to him. "WSM lost the dean of its Grand Ole Opry," he said. "His sterling character was appreciated by all who knew him, and especially the boys and girls who were associated with him on the program." Yet subsequent history has tended to overlook Dr. Bate's important role in starting the Opry; it was Dr. Bate who, even before Hay came to Nashville, saw the potential for using radio as a medium for country music. It was Dr. Bate whose vocation and reputation lent old-time music a much needed air of respectability. And it was Dr. Bate who, as much as anyone, gave to the Barn Dance a charming sense of informality and comradeship—a trait the modern Opry still endeavors to preserve. Because he was not a colorful or eccentric character like Uncle Dave Macon or Uncle Jimmy Thompson, Dr. Bate has not entered the folklore of the Opry; but he has a real and secure place in its history.

As the Barn Dance continued through 1926, some Nashville citizens grew alarmed at the show's success and of the image it was presenting of Nashville. A controversy arose over whether the old-time music should be replaced by modern popular music, and at one point a decision was made to temporarily suspend the Barn Dance broadcasts. But a flood of mail protesting the decision poured in, and the show stayed on the air. Hay said, "Much has been said for and against the old-time times but the fact remains that they are taking the country by storm. There is some delightful little folk strain that brings us all back to the soil, which runs through each of the numbers." A few years later Hay made this point even more emphatically: "In fact, we've been expecting that each year would be the last of this series [the Barn Dance]. . . . But we can't give it up. There's too much of a demand for the old folks and their tunes." Thus from its very earliest years, the Opry was aware of itself as a "folk music show," another trait the Opry tries to preserve even today— though the folk content of the show in the 1920s was considerably higher than that of today.

In fact, Hay began to emphasize more and more the "folk" aspect of the show. He cautioned his musicians about playing modern tunes or in modern styles; "Keep it down to earth, boys," became his byword. Soon he was constructing an image of the show that stressed its rustic, hayseed quality. He asked the musicians to stop wearing their business suits and instead to put on overalls and work shirts; publicity pictures were made of musicians in cornfields, with hound dogs, and jugs of moonshine. The Saturday night broadcasts were opened to an audience, and the radio show became in part a stage show. Hay attached colorful nicknames to his performers, names easily remembered by the audience; he gave wild, outlandish names to the string bands on the show. Thus Dr. Bate's band became the Possum Hunters, the Binkley Brothers String Orchestra became the Binkley Brothers Dixie Clodhoppers, and G.W. Wilkerson's band became the Fruit Jar Drinkers. A 1929 press release about the show emphasized that "every one of the 'talent' is from the back country" and the music on the show represents "unique entertainment that only the Tennessee mountaineers can afford." In truth, most of the early Opry musicians were from the Nashville area and worked at jobs as diverse as cigar makers, watch repairmen, and automobile mechanics; a few were farmers, but not many could accurately be described as "Tennessee mountaineers." It was in 1927 that Hay made the most important image

change: he renamed the show "Grand Ole Opry," in deliberate parody of the Grand Opera broadcasts then being enjoyed by the proper citizens of Nashville.

Other artists soon emerged to rival Uncle Dave, Dr. Bate, and Uncle Jimmy. Obed Pickard, a traveling salesman from Ashland City, became the first singing star of the show, specializing in old nineteenth-century songs like "Kitty Wells" and "Bury Me Not on the Lone Prairie." Pickard, who was billed as a "one-man orchestra," later formed the Pickard Family, which became one of the first family groups to broadcast country music nationwide over the NBC network. But by far the most popular solo performer on the pre-1930 Opry was a diminutive black man named Deford Bailey. Bailey, who was reared in a hamlet near Nashville, played solo harmonica; his specialties were "Fox Chase," in which he imitated dogs and hunters after the fox, and "Pan American Blues," a remarkable improvisation based on the sounds of a train that always passed near Deford's boyhood home. The novelty of the circumstance that Deford was the only black performer on an all-white hillbilly show should not obscure the fact that he was one of the most creative harmonica players in country music history. Much has been made of Deford's playing "blues" on the Opry, but a considerable portion of Deford's music was from hillbilly tradition; Deford himself calls his music "black hillbilly" music and points out that in his youth there were many black rural musicians playing old-time string band music. It is too easy today to call the music of every black musician "blues"; much of Deford's music was actually pre-blues music, and Deford is one of the few exemplars of this entire folk music tradition that is now almost extinct. But for whatever reason, Deford was vastly popular with Opry crowds, both on radio and in personal appearances. Although he was condescendingly labeled the "mascot" of the Opry, he remained an Opry mainstay until World War II.

Many early country performers considered recordings as much less important than radio work; as one early musician put it, "No one ever got rich off a record in those days, even if it was a hit. But radio—you could at least get regular pay out of it." This "regular pay" for the Opry began about 1928, and at first amounted only to about a dollar a minute, or $10–$15 a night for most artists. The low pay was satisfactory for most of the musicians because they were playing mainly as a hobby and had regular jobs during the week. But a

In 1926, when the "barn dance" was just starting, Dr. Humphrey Bate and his Possum Hunters posed in business suits (above), but by 1928 (below) they reflected George Hay's decision to create a rustic image for the program. Bate was first to play country music over Nashville radio.

new generation of musicians was emerging, and many of them expected to earn their living by performing on the Opry. Until that time the only really "professional" musician on the Opry had been Uncle Dave Macon, who still toured and recorded between broadcasts; but he would not be alone long.

WSM was quickly becoming a station of national status. In 1927 it increased its power to 5,000 watts and five years later got a clear-channel frequency and boosted its power to 50,000 watts. In spite of the sudden proliferation of radio stations, WSM could still easily be heard all over the eastern United States. It joined the newly formed NBC network and began broadcasting network shows—that is, except for Saturday nights. WSM continued to preempt the network shows on Saturday in favor of the Opry; this move in itself shows how popular the Opry was, and how much confidence WSM had in it. The one Saturday show that WSM simply could not resist was the popular "Amos n' Andy," and during the 1930s WSM simply interrupted the Opry to run "Amos n' Andy."

All these events accelerated the trend toward professionalization and commercialization of the Opry. About 1930 Harry Stone replaced Hay as station manager (though Hay continued to be the Opry announcer); Stone was cool, efficient, businesslike, and thoroughly professional. He saw that the show would have to attract full-time, professional acts, and he set about trying to make it possible for WSM to support full-time musicians. This was rather easy with "regular" musicians, who could play in local dance orchestras and even in the WSM studio orchestra; it was less easy to find full-time work around Nashville for country musicians. To facilitate this effort, Stone founded, about 1934, the Artists' Service Bureau to help promote tours and live performance bookings for Opry acts. He also hired a music librarian, Vito Pellettieri, to oversee the increasingly complex world of copyrights, performance rights, and publishing royalties. Pellettieri also helped devise ways to sell Opry time to "outside" sponsors—companies other than National Life. Within a few short years the Opry had gone from an informal, rather chaotic, picking and singing session to a smooth-running segmented radio show similar to that of today. One could accuse Stone and his fellow workers of d...troying an authentic folk music environment and replacing it with a world o. copyrights, contracts, and professional jealousies; but he did make it possible for country music artists to make a living at their work.

DeFord Bailey, the Opry's legendary black harmonica player, had to play his harmonica through a megaphone for it to be picked up by the old carbon mikes. The apparatus to his right was probably used to add sound effects to his "train" pieces like "Pan American Blues."

Thus the Opry got its first generation of professional musicians. It also began to attract musicians from outside the immediate area. Virtually all the early Opry musicians came from within a 100-mile radius of Nashville; most were from Middle Tennessee, a few from Kentucky. But in 1931 a singing trio called the Vagabonds joined the show and at once became one of the most popular acts. The Vagabonds (composed of Herald Goodman, Curt Poulton, and Dean Upson) represented a number of ''firsts'' for the Opry. They were the first full-time act from outside the South (they were all from the Midwest); they were established in show business before they joined the show; they were trained musicians, skilled in reading and arranging, and experienced in song publishing; and they were one of the first Opry acts also to appear on WSM's regular schedule of non-Opry shows. Furthermore, they saw themselves primarily as singers, not as instrumentalists; only one of them, Curt Poulton, played the guitar. Up until their coming, much of the Opry emphasis had been on string band music, with occasional vocals by artists such as Obed Pickard; the success of the Vagabonds heralded the shift toward vocal music that was to characterize country music throughout the next two decades. The Vagabonds sang in a very smooth, sophisticated harmonic style and did a number of ''heart'' songs, like their big hig, ''Lamp Lightin' Time in the Valley.'' Unlike many other Opry acts, the Vagabonds also recorded extensively, and, to protect their songs, they founded what was probably the first Nashville-based country music publishing firm, Old Cabin Music, in 1931.

Other experienced acts soon followed the Vagabonds to WSM. Veteran minstrel man Lasses White joined the cast, and presided for a time over a regular minstrel show. And from Kentucky came an act called Asher Sizemore and Little Jimmy, a father and small son who featured ''hearth and home songs.'' The Sizemores were very popular from about 1932 to 1942, and ''little Jimmy'' (who started singing professionally before he entered grade school) became the most popular pre-teen in the South, before the advent of Shirley Temple. The Sizemores used every possible means to professionalize their music: radio, tours, recordings, and the selling of songbooks. (''That little boy sold thousands of songbooks,'' recalled Judge Hay.)

It is ironic that the first surge of commercialization in country music came in the midst of the Great Depression. This made it doubly hard for struggling musicians to make ends meet. People were not used to paying more than 25 cents to see a live show, and record royalties were as low as one-fourth cent per record (as opposed to an average 1974 scale of 25 cents per LP). The Opry name at first did not guarantee a full house to a touring artist; in fact, when the first Opry tour went out in 1931, it was headed by Uncle Dave Macon, and was billed as ''Uncle Dave Macon and His Moonshiners,'' with not a word about the Opry. And the services involved in commercialization cost as well; an artist touring in the mid-1930s out of the WSM Bureau usually found that of his gate receipts, WSM took 15 percent for booking the tour, and his manager took another 20 percent for helping promote the tour. What musicians' unions there were at the time seldom recognized "pickers" as "real musicians," and promoters often took advantage of musicians' naïveté and good will. And to top it all off, travel was still both exhausting and time-consuming; most musicians had to travel by car over rough roads, in adverse weather, for hundreds of miles—and hope that an audience showed up for their performance. Most acts that were regular on the Opry were required to be back in Nashville every Saturday night.

Two acts dominated the Opry in the mid-1930s, and they combined the best aspects of the older folk traditions with the new creative professionalism. Both were professionally polished and musically exciting, and yet both retained direct ties with the rich southern folk culture that so impressed Cecil Sharp. These groups were the Delmore Brothers and the Dixieliners. The Delmores were the most popular vocal duo of the time, and the Dixieliners were the most popular string band of the time.

The Delmore Brothers, Alton and Rabon, were from northern Alabama. They joined the Opry in 1933 and almost immediately attracted national attention with two songs that became standards in country music: "Brown's Ferry Blues" and "Gonna Lay Down My Old Guitar." The Delmores sang rather softly in close, lilting harmonies that they learned in the gospel singing schools of northern Alabama and southern Tennessee. They became the first of the great brother duets that were to mark country music in the 1930s. Alton Delmore, the older brother, was one of the most creative songwriters in country music; he often experimented with shifting harmonies and tricky timing, and displayed more than a touch of blues influence. Toward the end of his life Alton wrote an autobiography in which he describes in detail the troubles he and Rabon had in trying to make it as full-time professionals in the 1930s. They frequently quarreled with the Opry over matters of bookings and salaries, and struggled valiantly to earn respectability for country music from mainstream entertainers. Both brothers could read and write music, and both were very much aware of the stereotyped image the music had in the 1930s. Alton recalled: "The people in the North accepted country and western music much sooner than people in the South. There are too many 'Southern aristocrats' in the South. They would listen to the 'Grand Ole Opry' on the sly and pretend to their friends of the upper bracket that they didn't listen at all." The Delmores finally left the Opry in 1938—and went on to have a long career on radio and on records—but they left their mark on the Opry, and even Alton

had to admit years later that to a performer in the 1930s in the South, being on the Opry represented "the Bible of radio achievement."

The Dixieliners came about in 1930 when the McGee Brothers, Sam and Kirk, joined forces with a Dickson County railroad lineman and fiddler named Arthur Smith. Sam and Kirk had earlier played on the Opry by themselves and with Uncle Dave Macon. Sam especially had the reputation of being one of the finest guitarists in the South. The McGees hailed from near Franklin, Tennessee, where Sam learned to play guitar from rural black musicians about 1920. Sam soon developed a unique "flat-top" style wherein he played both rhythm and melody simultaneously; his 1926 recording of an original piece called "Buck Dancer's Choice" was very popular and helped establish him as a major influence on folk guitar stylings. He was, in fact, probably the first rural white guitarist really to exploit the guitar as a solo instrument; before his appearance on the scene the guitar had been used mainly as an accompaniment to vocal or fiddle music. Even Maybelle Carter's famous lead runs were quite simple compared to what Sam was doing. Sam's brother Kirk was also a competent instrumentalist and fine singer, and both men had well established reputations by the time they met Arthur Smith in 1930. Smith, for his part, had played some on the early Opry with his brother but had not really impressed anyone to the extent that Sam had.

The Dixieliners began to play regularly on the Opry and to tour out of the Artists' Service Bureau. At a time when country music was becoming more popular and more slick, the Dixieliners insisted on playing pure old-time southern string band and fiddle music, with a minimum of novelty or modern numbers. Kirk McGee recalls: "Arthur didn't have a lot of showmanship at first. He was a very solemn fellow. But his fiddling impressed them. He just whipped it out and played and they sat up and listened." Smith popularized a long string of good fiddle numbers, many of which have gone into folk tradition and have become bluegrass standards. They include "Pig in the Pen," "Red Apple Rag," "Dickson County Blues," "Mocking Bird," "Lost Train Blues," and "More Pretty Girls Than One." On "Who's Gonna Shoe Your Pretty Little Feet," Arthur sang harmony with his fiddle, and his recording of "Beautiful Brown Eyes" (made with the Delmore Brothers) was one of the first big "crossover" hits: it received ratings on both country music and popular best-seller lists. A number of modern fiddling scholars give Smith

The Gully Jumpers (top), one of the first Opry string bands, included, from left, Burt Hutcherson, Roy Hardison, Charlie Arrington, and the leader Paul Warmack. In the Opry's first tour group (bottom), in 1931, were Sam McGee and Uncle Dave Macon, seated; and, from left, Kirk McGee, Dr. Humphrey Bate, Dorris Macon, Buster Bate, Alcyone Bate, and Lou Hesson.

credit for popularizing the "long bow" technique throughout the South, and even today Arthur Smith's tunes and Arthur Smith's style can be heard at contests throughout the Southeast. Smith's fiddling influence, combined with Sam's guitar prowess, made the Dixieliners one of the most important string bands in country music history. Unfortunately, the band never recorded in its prime, though its members recorded separately; this is another example of how inaccurately phonograph records can reflect the development of country music. The band broke up in 1938 when Arthur left to go to Hollywood to play in western pictures. In the late 1950s folksinger Mike Seeger reunited the McGees and Smith and helped them stage a comeback during the folk revival of the 1960s. Today Kirk McGee, who still plays on the Opry, is the only surviving member of the Dixieliners.

In the 1930s the advent of cowboy music and western swing helped country music gain a broader national audience, and the Opry reflected these new musical forms. Western swing utilized amplified instruments, jazz rhythms, improvised solos, and even drums, and the Opry soon could boast of acts like Zeke Clements and his Bronco Busters, a western band which featured Texas Ruby Owens, "Radio's Original Yodelling Cowgirl." Pee Wee King's Golden West Cowboys was the first group regularly to use an electric guitar (though Sam McGee had tried unsuccessfully to introduce one earlier). Slim Smith specialized in western songs, and Jack Shook's Missouri Mountaineers helped expand instrumentation beyond the basic fiddle, banjo, and guitar. Still other performers found they could specialize exclusively in comedy, and a tradition of rustic humor, drawing from old vaudeville and medicine show routines, was born. Lasses White and Honey Wilds did a blackface routine, and Edna Wilson and Margaret Waters endeared themselves to radio audiences by portraying two old mountain women named Sarie and Sally. Robert Lunn, from Franklin, Tennessee, did comedy songs like "Tooth Pickin' Time in False Teeth Valley" and helped popularize the "Talking Blues," a form to be later used by folksinger Woody Guthrie and his followers.

The days when Opry performers were drawn exclusively from the Middle Tennessee area were gone by the 1930s, but Tennessee as a whole continued to provide a steady stream of fresh talent for the show. In spite of the growing numbers of smooth professionals on the show and the noticeable western

Most popular string band of the mid-30s, the Dixieliners (top), included, from left, Sam McGee, Arthur Smith, and Kirk McGee. Roy Acuff, the "king of country music," and his band pose in 1938 (bottom), shortly after joining the Opry from Knoxville. From left, members are Oswald Kirby, Jess Easterly Acuff, comedienne Rachel Veach, and Lonnie (Pap) Wilson.

influence in the late 1930s, the most single important addition to the Opry during this time was a singer who "brought it back home" to the basics of good old-time mountain music: Roy Acuff. When Acuff joined the Opry in early 1938, he became popular almost immediately, and he has managed to retain this popularity through the 1970s. Today he is recognized as "the king of country music" and his name has become almost synonymous with that of the Grand Ole Opry itself. It is possible to think of an Opry without Roy Acuff, but it would be a strange, characterless affair. Acuff from the first reemphasized the old-time singing style of the East Tennessee hills and later fought to preserve the dignity and worth of southern country music against the onslaughts of western and popular music. He became the Opry's first real solo star after Uncle Dave Macon, and proved to be one of its main links with tradition.

Acuff was born in Maynardville, Tennessee, in 1903, though he spent much of his early life in Fountain City, at that time a suburb of Knoxville. His father was a Baptist preacher who taught his son to love both sacred music and fiddle music. Acuff recalls: "Many, many times back in Maynardsville, when I was just a kid, in the real cold winter nights and the mornings when father would get out of bed when the house was warming up after he had built the fires, he would take the old fiddle out from under the bed and play it up there in the hollow . . . it built something in me that I have never forgotten." The Acuff family also sang a lot, and Roy remembers singing old broadside ballads like "The Sinking of the Titanic." Yet as a boy Acuff showed little outstanding musical talent, and planned to become a baseball player.

For about five years Acuff had a rather successful career playing ball, but his playing days ended in 1929 when he suffered a severe sunstroke. As it became obvious that he would not play any more ball, he began to practice the fiddle; he would listen to records on the Victrola by champion East Tennessee fiddler Uncle Am Stuart, along with Fiddlin' John Carson and Gid Tanner. He tried to learn the old fiddle tunes off the Victrola, but "it was hard to find out what key they were playing in, because you had the wind-up Victrola, and the faster it played the higher it was pitched, and I never could know whether I was in standard or what they were doing." Soon he joined a medicine show and toured East Tennessee, singing, acting in the old skits, and helping to sell "Mocatan tonic. . . . I got to play every type of character. I got to play the blackface part back then, and got to play the little girl's part . . . and I'd play the Toby part." (The Toby was a clown role common to most rural medicine shows.) "Then I'd play the fiddle and sing. I'd sing real loud on the med show, sing where they could hear me a long ways." Acuff soon developed a singing style quite different from many of the country singers of the day.

"They used to talk about the nasal voice until I came along. I was one of the first who ever put a real strong voice in country music."

By 1934 Acuff had formed a string band that was playing regularly on Knoxville station WROL; an announcer casually dubbed the group the Crazy Tennesseans, and the name stuck. Acuff was still as much of a fiddler as he was a singer, and he often shared vocal chores with other members of his band. But the band's popularity grew, and Acuff began to further professionalize his music. On one Knoxville show he was getting a meager 50 cents per show, and he recalls dreaming of the time when he could "play a date where the box office receipts would total as much as one hundred dollars." A step toward this goal came in 1936 when his group was invited to record for the American Record Corporation. In two sessions the band recorded over thirty sides, many of which were chosen for mail order distribution by Sears, Roebuck and Company. Among these was a sacred song called "The Great Speckle Bird" [sic], which Roy had learned from another Knoxville band in 1935; the song had become his most famous radio number, and it became an immensely popular record. (The title of the song comes from Jeremiah 12:9, where the speckled bird is a symbol of the Bible.) The song was so popular, in fact, that Acuff recorded a sequel to it ("Great Speckle Bird #2") a few months later. Other recordings from this first session reflected the mixed repertoire of the band: there were traditional East Tennessee folk songs like "Charmin' Betsy," "All Night Long," and "Greenback Dollar"; a few popular numbers like "Yes, Sir, That's My Baby" and "You've Gotta See Mama Every Night"; and a couple of slightly off-color pieces, such as "Doing It the Old Fashioned Way," which were issued under the pseudonym "The Bang Boys." Two other songs in the session were destined to become among Acuff's most popular: "Freight Train Blues" and "Wabash Cannonball." Ironically, Acuff did not sing on this first version of "Wabash Cannonball," a tune that was to become his theme song in later years; Dynamite Hatcher, the band's harmonica player, sang the original vocal on the song, while Roy did the train imitations.

By this time Roy was writing regularly to Judge Hay trying to get on the Opry. His recording success did not impress the WSM managers, though; they still considered the band too rough and primitive. Finally, when Arthur Smith was temporarily suspended from the Opry, Hay needed a substitute and gave the Acuff band a chance. There was not much response to Roy's fiddling, but his singing of "Great Speckle Bird" struck home; the next week Opry officials were looking at sacks of fan mail praising the new singer. Harry Stone, the station manager, thought the band name "Crazy Tennesseans" was undignified, and renamed the group "The Smoky Mountain Boys." (It was a sign of the times that by 1938 Stone was reversing Hay's earlier habit of attaching "hayseed" names to the groups; it shows how far the music, and the Opry, had come in one short decade.) By 1939 Acuff was the most popular singer on the program and was attracting new national attention to the Opry.

In fact, Acuff helped to make 1939 a watershed year for the Opry. The NBC network finally decided to carry a half hour of the Opry on Saturday night, thus giving national exposure to the music and the artists; people around the country now did not have to listen through the static to distant WSM, but could hear the show piped through their local network station. (Of course, many continued to endure the static for those three and a half hours of Opry music *not* on the network.) But the Opry image was glorified even more by the release that year of a Hollywood film, "The Grand Ole Opry," which featured Roy Acuff in a leading role. Other Opry regulars appeared in the picture, including Judge Hay himself and Uncle Dave Macon. To Hollywood, the picture was probably just another medium-budget musical and was certainly nothing on the scope of that year's masterpiece, "The Wizard of Oz." The plot was contrived and the jokes corny, but this picture did much for country music. At a time when the films were full of cowboys singing western music, this film asserted the validity of southern music. In the film, the hero is a small-town mayor who decides to reform the big city politics, and he gets elected through his use of country music in the campaign. He succeeds, and "Grand Ole Opry music" (as it is called) emerges as the "music of the people." It is pictured as honest, open music that reflects the simple, conservative values of rural America. The fact that such a film could be made indicates the degree of acceptability that country music had, not only across Tennessee but across the nation. Indeed, country music was now ready for its final thrust into the mainstream of American pop music.

4. Honky-Tonk, Tuxedoes, and Bluegrass

During the latter days of World War II a story was circulating among the musicians in downtown Nashville. The story took several different forms, depending on who was telling it, but the basic kernel was the same: while stationed on the Pacific island of Okinawa, a Marine detachment endured a number of Japanese banzai attacks. Before the attack, the Japanese would try to "psych out" the Marines by yelling taunts at them. Prior to one particular attack, the Americans heard the Japanese yelling: "To hell with President Roosevelt! To hell with Babe Ruth! To hell with Roy Acuff!"

This story may be folklore, but it illustrates a telling point: near the end of World War II, Acuff had become a significant national hero, not just a regional one. And, by extension, the music Acuff represented had gained national appeal. During the war, southerners found themselves stationed in all parts of the country and around the world, and they took their country music with them. Fellow soldiers from the North and Midwest who had been raised on the music of Bing Crosby and Frank Sinatra were exposed to the music of Roy Acuff, Pee Wee King, and Bob Wills. The servicemen heard it from the juke boxes in the cafes and post exchanges; they heard it from fellow soldiers who found that a guitar was a simple and easily transportable instrument. The army itself helped spread the music through its own radio network; AFRS (Armed Forces Radio Service) transcriptions (the forerunners of LP records) of stateside radio shows were mailed to bases around the world, and these shows included a number of country music shows. By 1944 a half-hour Opry show was being syndicated through AFRS channels, with the announcer being careful to specify that the music was "American folk music or music in the folk style." ("Folk music" was a term thought more respectable than "hill-billy" or "country": ironically, it was being applied at a time when much of the genuine folk content of the music was vanishing.) Soldiers also heard their share of live country music. In late 1941, Nashville promoter J.L. Frank, along with Opry manager Harry Stone, organized a regular series of country music tours to stateside military bases. The tour was called the Camel Caravan (in tribute to the sponsor's product, Camel cigarettes), and it included about twenty entertainers from the Opry cast, including Pee Wee King, Eddy Arnold, and comedienne Minnie Pearl. The tours were astoundingly successful; by late 1942 the Camel Caravan had gone more than 50,000 miles in nineteen states and had played 175 shows in 68 different army camps, field hospitals, airfields, and bases. Later other Opry entertainers continued to make tours for servicemen, even after the war. The armed forces in World War II served as a giant melting pot of various ethnic and geographical traditions, and country music became a prime ingredient.

Many southerners who did not go to war found themselves caught up in the population shifts caused by the war: rural southerners had been gradually moving into the North, Midwest, and West in order to find work in the factories and plants there, and the war accelerated this trend. The typical country music fan found himself caught up in a modern, industrialized world full of tensions and anxieties. Sentimental songs about mother and home, event songs like "The Death of Floyd Collins," and old murder ballads had little to say to a factory worker worried about car payments, a drinking problem, or an impending divorce. A new type of country song was born, a song which reflected this modern society and its problems; the new song was essentially a form poets would call a "lyric lament." It was nearly always a first-person, highly subjective account, and nearly always was about lost or unrequited love. One of the first big song hits of this variety on the Grand Ole Opry was sung by a young singer from Texas, a pupil of blue yodeler Jimmie Rodgers (who also pioneered such laments), named Ernest Tubb. Tubb's song, which became a country standard and earned Tubb a permanent berth on the Opry, was "I'm Walkin' the Floor Over You."

Tubb's brand of music was labelled "honky-tonk" because it was a style that originated in Texas beer halls and roadhouses of that name. Along with lyrics that described "troubles" and drinking, the music soon developed a distinct style based on the electric steel guitar, the use of "sock" chords on the rhythm guitar, the string bass, the use of the fiddle and piano as backup instruments, and a steady, danceable rhythm. The style dominated country music in the late 1940s and 1950s, and by the 1970s it was being referred to as "mainstream" country music. The "honky-tonk" style has, in fact, proven to be one of the most enduring styles in American popular music.

Although honky-tonk style originated in the Southwest, many Tennessee musicians soon integrated it into their music. One of the earliest and most successful singers to do this was Carl Smith, a singer from Roy Acuff's hometown of Maynardville, Tennessee. Smith sang in a full-voiced mountain style like Acuff, but used the newer instrumentation of the honky-tonk tradition. Where Acuff stressed his East Tennessee mountain heritage, Smith cultivated a cowboy image: he wore western clothes, cowboy boots, and lived on a ranch near Nashville. Starting his career on Knoxville radio, Smith enjoyed early success with hit records like "Hey, Joe" and "Let Old Mother Nature Have Her Way." He joined the Opry in 1950, and in 1952–1953 won a string of national awards, including the *Cash Box* award for "Best Folk Artist." Although he featured a number of western songs, such as Bob Wills's "Time Changes Everything," Smith often returned to the music of his East Tennessee heritage. He recorded, for instance, with the Carter Family. Later in 1959, he produced a hit, "Ten Thousand Drums," which was a "saga song" written in the mold of the old ballads collected by Cecil Sharp. Other Tennessee singers who successfully built careers on honky-tonk tradition include Carl Butler, from Knoxville, who used honky-tonk instrumentation to back a vocal style heavily influenced by white gospel music of the Southeast. Butler's biggest success was a song called "Don't Let Me Cross Over" (1963), but he had earlier recorded many sacred numbers including "Angel Band," "Looking through the Windows of Heaven," and "Walking in God's Sunshine." Butler, in fact, anticipated much of the tenor of modern white gospel music with his mixture of sacred and secular forms. Even more recently Jack Greene, of Maryville, Tennessee, a veteran of years playing with Ernest Tubb's band, has continued to carry on the purer honky-tonk tradition at the Opry.

But the man who did most for making honky-tonk music the dominant style came not from Tennessee but from Alabama: Hank Williams. Williams' influence on country music of the 1950s was as great as that of Jimmie Rodgers in the 1930s, and like Rodgers, Williams had a brief meteoric career filled with personal tragedy. And, like Rodgers, Williams became a sort of culture hero to millions of fans who held his life, and what he stood for, to be as interesting as his music. Coming from Georgiana, Alabama, where he learned much of his early style from an old black street singer, Williams came to Nashville in the late 1940s as a song writer. He teamed with Roy Acuff's publishing partner, Fred Rose, and began to record as well as write songs. His first release, "Move It On Over," became a hit, and later songs like "Cold, Cold Heart," "Lovesick Blues," and "Your Cheatin' Heart" helped Williams move from the Louisiana Hayride onto the stage of the Grand Ole Opry. Here he continued to produce an impressive string of original songs, the most famous of which were love ballads like "I'm So Lonesome I Could Cry," and "I Can't Help It if I'm Still in Love with You." However, he also wrote sacred songs like "I Saw the Light" and "When God Comes and Gathers His Jewels," and even novelty songs like "Jambalaya" and "Kaw-Liga," the latter a droll masterpiece about a wooden Indian who falls in love. Williams usually sang his own songs in a rough-sounding nasal voice that had more than a touch of the blues in it. Williams' fans saw in his songs a reflection of the turbulence that marked his personal life; he had a serious drinking problem which got worse as his life became more complicated. He was fired from the Opry in August 1952 because of his drinking, and within six months he was dead. Within an effective performing career of less than five years, Williams crystalized the direction country music was to take for the next twenty years.

Because of his unprecedented popularity, Williams found himself often performing in places normally reserved for mainstream popular singers. Once, in Louisville, he even upstaged famed comedian Bob Hope. The lessons of his popularity were not lost on the pop singers of the day; eight of his hits were "covered" in pop versions by mainstream singers, and one of these cover versions, Tony Bennett's version of "Cold, Cold Heart," sold one and a half million copies. Williams was by no means the first country singer to have his songs covered by pop singers—Bing Crosby covered Tubb's "Walkin' the Floor Over You" and Bob Wills's "San Antonio Rose" in the early 1940s—but the success of his songs exemplified yet another important development in country music: its increasing appeal to non-country audiences. By the end of World War II it was obvious that a country song could be a "crossover" hit—that it could appeal both to country and popular audiences. This encouraged some country artists to move in yet another direction, toward a more urban, smooth, sophisticated sound. At the same time that honky-tonk was reasserting country music's rough, folksy vitality, an "uptown" brand of country music was expanding the popularity of the music even beyond the success of the Grand Ole Opry. Yet the hills of Tennessee continued to produce talent for even this newer brand of music as well, and the careers of two Tennessee musicians could be read as case histories of how country music moved from the overalls and the cowboy costumes of the Opry to the tuxedoes of Carnegie Hall. These musicians are Eddy Arnold and Tennessee Ernie Ford.

Born on a farm near Henderson, Tennessee, in 1918, Eddy Arnold came from a family of sharecroppers; he learned to play with a Sears mail-order guitar and soon was broadcasting over WTJS in Jackson, Tennessee, and later in Memphis, Louisville, and St. Louis. When he was eighteen, he joined Pee

This 1949 performance by Minnie Pearl represented one of many tours by the Opry to military bases during and after World War II. The popular singers Tennessee Ernie Ford (left) and Eddy Arnold were pioneers in merging country and pop music in the early 1950s.

Wee King's Golden West Cowboys as a vocalist specializing in songs with a western flavor. King's band was a rather sophisticated unit which utilized such nontraditional instruments as the electric steel guitar, the accordian, and drums, and Arnold began to form a singing style suited to this expanded accompaniment. In 1944 he left King and, calling himself "The Tennessee Plowboy," began to perform six days a week over WSM. Arnold had a warm, clear baritone voice which he shrewdly framed with a achingly pure steel guitar accompaniment by Roy Wiggins. He began to record for RCA Victor, then emerging as one of the country's top companies, and in the late 1940s enjoyed numerous best-selling records: "That's How Much I Love You," "Bouquet of Roses," "It's a Sin," and later, "Cattle Call." Arnold soon replaced Acuff as country music's most popular singer; by 1947, barely a year after Arnold gained wide popularity, his record company announced that he had sold over 2,700,000 records. As his popularity increased, Arnold by 1948 was continuing to modify his style even more toward an urbane, "crooning" delivery, and he actively sought engagements in night clubs and supper clubs throughout the country. Under the direction of his promoter, Colonel Tom Parker (who later was to manage an equally successful crossover performer, Elvis Presley), Arnold phased out his "Tennessee Plowboy" image and cultivated an image of black ties and tuxedoes. He was soon appearing on national television with stars such as Milton Berle, Arthur Godfrey, Perry Como, and Bob Hope, and in a short time he had his own national show. Later Arnold became one of the first country singers to do a show at Carnegie Hall. Yet under Parker's genius Arnold managed to hold onto much of his country audience while adding fans from the ranks of businessmen, professionals, and bankers. Today Arnold is recognized as often as a pop singer as he is a country singer, and it was for this breakthrough as much as anything that Arnold was elected to the Country Music Hall of Fame in 1966.

Even more successful than Arnold at converting his country style into pop style is Tennessee Ernie Ford. Ford was born in 1919 near Bristol, in the heart of the Appalachian folk ballad region Sharp so successfully documented. As a boy he was exposed to the genuine folk music of the area, and to the Methodist hymns sung by his kinfolk; however, he aspired to become an opera singer and took vocal training. He broadcast over WOPI in Bristol and WNOX in Knoxville before entering service for World War II. Moving to California after the war, he began appearing on radio and television; his formal music training made it easier for him to move toward popular music, and by 1953 he was appearing on a national non-country TV show. His singing style was continuing to move toward a compromise of country and pop; Ford recalled, "You know I couldn't top Roy Acuff's stuff, and I couldn't beat [Perry] Como. So I mix 'em and people like it fine.'' He soon had his own national radio show and was recording with pop singers like Kay Starr. Ford's early hits—for example, ''Mule Train'' and ''Shotgun Boogie''—had country flavor but featured Ford's strong, non-nasal baritone with modern instrumentation. By 1955 Ford had so successfully adapted to pop that one music historian reported he had ''by this time left the country music field.'' Yet in that same year Ford had his biggest hit, a recording of ''Sixteen Tons,'' a coal-mining protest song based partly on genuine tradition and partly on a composition by Kentucky guitarist Merle Travis. This song's success made Ford a national figure, but his recordings continued to have country flavor—even in modern orchestrations. One of his first LP albums featured genuine folk songs like ''Rovin' Gambler,'' and in 1956 Ford began recording a series of albums of hymns and spirituals which became among the most popular produced by any singer, country or not. In the 1970s Ford reinforced his ties with the country audience by associating himself with the Nashville scene; he began to record country material again, and he toured Russia with a country music show drawn from Nashville's Opry and Opryland (see chapter 5).

Arnold and Ford did not just see their songs move into pop circles; they themselves became pop entertainers and pioneered the way for later country singers who sought to expand the dimensions of their music. The possibilities of such expansion was shown by yet another event of the early 1950s: the popularity of a song called ''The Tennessee Waltz.'' This song was originally written in 1947 by singer Redd Stewart and his bandleader Pee Wee King. Stewart, a native of Ashland City, Tennessee, had been inspired to write the song by the success of a similar song by Bill Monroe entitled ''The Kentucky Waltz.'' Stewart first sang the familiar lyric (''I was waltzing with my darling / To the Tennessee Waltz'') over Louisville radio about 1948, and it was soon recorded by a country duo, the Short Brothers, and by dance band leader Erskine Hawkins. The song was popular but then faded into obscurity. Then, in 1959, a *Billboard* staff writer named Jerry Wexler suggested that a young pop singer named Patti Page use the song as the ''B'' side of her new record. She did, and by December 1950 the song had become the most popular in the nation; within six months ''The Tennessee Waltz,'' in its original and cover versions, had sold nearly 5,000,000 records. Historian Bill Malone reports: ''It was generally believed that 'The Tennessee Waltz' was the biggest hit in modern popular-music history. . . .'' The song has gone on to become a country standard; in 1965 it was adopted as the official Tennessee state anthem. Stewart had published the song with Acuff-Rose, a prominent Nashville music firm, and the song's success in northern music circles made the Nashville music publishing industry aware of the crossover potential for their product. More than any other single country song of the time, ''The Tennessee Waltz'' anticipated the way in which country music was to become a major American cultural force. Allen Churchill, writing in the *New York Times Magazine* in 1951, remarked, ''New York's writers of pop tunes look in envy and calculation at the 'country' songsmiths. . . . There's a revolution brewing in the music business.''

Yet if there was a revolution brewing in Nashville in the early 1950s, there was in other parts of Tennessee a movement back to the roots of country music. It was a movement that rejected modern electric instruments in favor of country music's basic string group of the guitar, fiddle, and banjo. It was a movement also that took the banjo, which had become virtually extinct in modern country music, and raised it to a prominent position; that emphasized the high, lonesome vocal sound of the East Tennessee mountains instead of the smooth, crooning sound of Eddy Arnold; and that returned to the older folk songs and folk themes of home, sentiment, and lost love instead of modern themes of betrayal, drinking, and self-doubt. The movement took its name from the band formed by a Kentucky mandolin player named Bill Monroe: bluegrass.

It would be wrong to see bluegrass as only a revival of traditional southern string band styles; there were a number of important differences. In the traditional string band, the fiddle usually dominated the banjo and guitar; in bluegrass, the banjo became a lead instrument, and other musicians often took solos, much in the manner of members of a jazz band. The mandolin, seldom played in old-time bands, took a regular role in the bluegrass band, and the dobro (an unamplified steel guitar) was frequently used. But the most significant innovation of bluegrass music was the use of a revolutionary banjo-picking style, a rolling, three-finger style known as ''Scruggs style.'' This style originated in the mountains of North Carolina and was popularized by Earl Scruggs. It was a style that enabled the banjoist to produce a rapid stream of notes and to accentuate the melody line by embroidering it with hundreds of sparkling grace notes. An ideal style for a lead instrument, it allowed the bluegrass band to take numbers at breakneck tempos that were two or even three times faster than traditional sting band tempos.

It has become customary to refer to Bill Monroe as ''the father of bluegrass music.'' Although he was born in Kentucky and achieved his first real

Singer Redd Stewart (top) co-authored with Pee Wee King the famous hit, ''The Tennessee Waltz.'' The bluegrass movement in country music took its name from Bill Monroe, shown below with his 1946 band: from left, Birch Monroe, Chubby Wise, Monroe, Lester Flatt, and Earl Scruggs.

professional success in the Carolinas, Bill Monroe first defined bluegrass music as it is known today from the stage of Nashville's Grand Ole Opry. Monroe had enjoyed considerable success in the late 1930s with a duet act featuring himself and his brother Charlie; the two split in 1938, and Bill formed a band called the Blue Grass Boys (after the nickname of his native state). The band joined the Opry in 1939 and was moderately successful, but for the next six years the band employed a style that was not all that different from other string bands of the era. In 1945, however, the Blue Grass Boys underwent a major change; three men joined the band who were to give it a radically different sound: fiddler Chubby Wise, guitarist and singer Lester Flatt, and banjoist Earl Scruggs. Wise was a Florida fiddler who was skilled in playing in a hard-driving, bluesy style that owed as much to western swing as it did to old-time mountain fiddling. His playing both with Monroe and later by himself helped define the style of bluegrass fiddling; he helped compose perhaps the most popular bluegrass fiddle number, "Orange Blossom Special." Flatt, the only Tennessee native in the trio, was born in 1914 in Overton County and learned to play from his parents, who both played banjo in the old-time "frailing" style. After an apprenticeship playing music in Virginia, Flatt and his wife both joined Charlie Monroe's band; a couple of years later he came to Nashville to join Bill Monroe. Flatt had an influential guitar style and his famous "G run" became a standard way to open and begin choruses in bluegrass music. The Flatt vocal style, which has been described as having "the easygoing lilt of a rural Bing Crosby," complemented Monroe's singing perfectly. The third member of the trio, Earl Scruggs, was a North Carolina native who brought out of the hills the fluid Scruggs banjo style described above. Scruggs supposedly discovered his own particular variation of the three-finger style when, at age ten, he was playing the banjo to cool off after an argument with his brother. He just stumbled onto the technique and for a time was upset because his banjo playing did not sound just like that of other pickers in the area. But he decided to live with it and took comfort in the fact that he could play almost any kind of tune in the style. By 1945, when he was twenty-one, Scruggs joined a Knoxville band headed by a popular regional fiddler, "Lost John" Miller. After playing around Knoxville for some months, Miller decided to disband his outfit, and Scruggs was out of a job. Several people were urging Scruggs to try to get on with Monroe. As Monroe recalls, "I had three appointments with Earl, and I missed the first two, and the third one I went down to where he was at. . . . So when I heard Earl, I knew that that banjo picking would fit my music. . . . He could help take lead breaks like the fiddle, and would be a great help to me." Before Scruggs joined, Monroe had used the banjo primarily as a rhythm instrument. Now Scruggs used it to rip off lead runs, and veterans of the time recall how the crowds at the Opry went wild when they first heard Scruggs playing. In fact, with three major creative genuises added to its ranks, Bill Monroe's Blue Grass Boys soon became one of the most influential string bands in the country.

This band was also popular on the Opry, and toured widely. It also recorded, and bluegrass historians give it credit for recording, in 1946, the first true bluegrass record, "Will You Be Loving Another Man" (with a Flatt vocal) backed with "Blue Yodel No. 4," an old Jimmie Rodgers tune. The 1945 band recorded only fourteen records (twenty-eight songs), but they included Scruggs specialties like "Molly and Tenbrooks" (a Kentucky folksong about a horse race) and "Blue Grass Breakdown." The 1945 band became the prototype of all later bluegrass bands, but it existed in an environment—the postwar Opry—that was geared to the more modern sounds of honky-tonk and country crooning. On the Opry, Scruggs was introduced as "the boy from North Carolina who makes the banjo talk"—a rather condescending phrase that implied Scruggs was some sort of trick banjoist instead of the most important instrumentalist of his generation. Both Flatt and Scruggs tired of the hectic touring, and in 1948, after three years with Monroe, both quit and formed their own band. Significantly, they did not stay in Nashville, but returned to East Tennessee, where their music found an even more congenial reception.

East Tennessee, in fact, soon became a center for bluegrass music. Though WSM continued to dominate mainstream country music with the Opry, there was little other country music on the station; during the 1940s WSM was busy developing popular programs for NBC and building an image as a major national station. The radio stations in East Tennessee were far more receptive to new country shows, in part because they did not have the network obligations of WSM. And the East Tennessee stations were more receptive to the more traditional, "purer" forms of country music because they did not have to please such a wide and diverse audience; many listeners in the hills of East Tennessee still liked the old styles and the old songs. Also, by the end of the war the technology was available that would allow independent radio stations and record companies to develop apart from the national networks and big record companies and to produce a specific product for a specific audience. Bluegrass was just such a product. Its development in East Tennessee can be attributed to three main factors: the radio stations in Knoxville, the radio activity in the Bristol–Johnson City area, and a pioneering record company formed in Johnson City.

From the mid-1930s to the 1950s two stations dominated the music scene in Knoxville, WNOX and WROL. Two colorful personalities dominated these two stations: Lowell Blanchard over WNOX and Cas Walker over WROL. Blanchard was a part-time singer and song writer, but he primarily acted as master of ceremonies for a daily one-hour noon show called "The Mid-Day Merry-Go-Round." Walker was a local grocer who found out early that he could sell a lot of groceries by sponsoring country music shows. (Walker still sponsors a daily country music show over Knoxville television.) There was rivalry between WNOX and WROL, but it was a friendly rivalry that never got out of hand. Walker recalls an anecdote that shows how much the two men dominated their stations. "People would burn their tubes out, their radio tubes out. . . . There was one we called the Cas Walker tube, and one called the Lowell Blanchard tube. . . . They'd burn out one, we'd say the Lowell Blanchard tube was burned out, they'd burned out [his] but could still get me. They burned out mine, they could still get him, we'd have it the Cas Walker tube had burned out."

Guitarist Chet Atkins was one who got his start playing over WNOX, and he recalled the scene there in the early 1940s: "At WNOX there were more than 150 half-hour programs a week, most of them country music." Atkins himself played with a number of musicians, including Archie Campbell and Bill Carlisle, who later went to Nashville. The comedy team of "Homer" Haynes and Jethro Burns, later to become famous for their parodies of country songs, were from Knoxville and often appeared on WNOX. In fact, the Knoxville stations often drew from local talent, and many native Tennesseans who later went on to careers in music got started on WNOX. One musician playing in the area at the time recalls that the "Mid-Day Merry-Go-Round" was "often a stepping stone to the Grand Ole Opry." Certainly the Opry's most famous star, Acuff, was an alumnus of the program. In the late 1940s the show helped launch the career of Johnnie and Jack (Johnnie Wright and Jack Anglin), who were the country's most popular brother duo until Anglin's untimely death in a car wreck in the early 1950s. (Also performing with Johnnie and Jack at Knoxville was Kitty Wells, who became one of the music's first successful female stars with her recording of "It Wasn't God Who Made Honky-Tonk Angels" in 1952.) Other popular performers on WNOX included bass player Smilin' Eddie Hill, who was often active in early bluegrass music, and a blackface comedian named Kentucky Slim, who delighted audiences in live performances with a medicine show routine called "the pork chop dance."

Knoxville grocer Cas Walker is shown (top) with his 1937 band on WROL. Standing, from left, are Walker, Kentucky Slim Henry Brown, and unidentified fiddler; seated are Hubert Davenport, Bob Darnell, and Cal Davenport. Below, Guitarist Chet Atkins (here with fiddle!) is one of the stars who launched careers over Knoxville's WNOX. In this 1944 appearance, he is with Johnny Wright, left, and Kitty Wells and Eddie Hill.

On Cas Walker's show on WROL the bluegrass was a little thicker. Cas called bluegrass "jumping up and down music," and he explained his rationale for using it on his shows. "If you have what I call jumping up and down music, bluegrass, and something that a child can jump up and down to, you make the children jump up and down and listen to you, and when you please someone's child, you please the papa and mama. . . . every child knows Cas Walker, and that's not bad, when everyone is going to be eating at one time or another." It was WROL that Lester Flatt and Earl Scruggs chose to use as their broadcasting base after they left Bill Monroe, and for a time they toured out of Knoxville. Other bluegrass musicians that passed through Cas Walker's show make up a Who's Who of early bluegrass: the Brewster Brothers, the Cope Brothers, the Webster Brothers, and even the Osborne Brothers, a Kentucky duo who went on to become prime innovators of new bluegrass forms. One of the most popular groups was the Bailey Brothers, a remarkable duo whose music represented an important transitional link between the close-harmony duet singing of the 1930s and the newer bluegrass forms. Danny and Charles Bailey were both from the hamlet of Klondike, Tennessee (in the northeast corner of the state), and by 1940 they were appearing regularly for Cas Walker on WROL. They did a great many older sentimental songs, as well as gospel material, and were often joined on some numbers by their announcer, the then-unknown Tennessee Ernie Ford. The Baileys' popularity in those days was immense, and for a time they were doing four radio shows a day in addition to personal appearances at night. In the mid-1940s the boys had a brief stint with the Opry in Nashville and experimented with a modern steel guitar, but they soon abandoned the steel guitar, left the Opry, and returned to East Tennessee. They continued to play through the area into the 1950s and worked with many of the important bluegrass instrumentalists of the day. In the 1970s the Baileys were reunited and performed widely, being hailed by a new generation of bluegrass fans as the important pioneers they were.

Further east, in Johnson City, station WJHL went on the air in the late 1930s, with broadcasting studios at both Johnson City and Elizabethton. Although the station broadcast a number of independent country shows, its most successful was a program called "Barrel of Fun." This program resembled in many ways what the Opry had been in its early years: an informal

Station WOPI *in Johnson City was an important center for country music after 1930. From the station's control room (top), pictured here in the mid-30s, was broadcast the popular "Saturday Night Jamboree," which was held in* WOPI's *350-seat Radiotorium (bottom).*

gathering of all sorts of amateur pickers and singers. "Barrel of Fun" was broadcast live from a theater in Elizabethton for two and a half hours every Saturday morning and was managed by a colorful local personality named "Turtle" Tolbert. "Barrel of Fun" produced no real superstars, but the show did reinforce the audience's love of traditional music.

In nearby Bristol, station WOPI began broadcasting in 1929 and soon had a number of popular live country music shows originating from its "Radiotorium"—a combination auditorium and studio. Many of the traditional musicians of the Bristol area who had recorded in the 1920s, Charlie Bowman and the Roe Brothers, for example, appeared on this important early station. By the late 1940s, though, another Bristol station, WCYB, was showcasing some of the best early bluegrass music. Three of the most important bluegrass bands—Flatt and Scruggs, the Stanley Brothers, and Carl Story—gained early exposure on WCYB. Story popularized "bluegrass gospel" music, and Carter and Ralph Stanley, originally from Virginia, had one of the first bands to play in the Bill Monroe style; the Stanleys were responsible for popularizing smoother, more sophisticated bluegrass vocal styles. For a time in 1948 the Stanley Brothers appeared on a two-hour daily show called "Farm and Fun Time" alongside Lester Flatt and Earl Scruggs and their new band, the Foggy Mountain Boys. Ralph Stanley, who had grown up playing the older claw-hammer style of mountain banjo, took this opportunity to learn to play the newer three-finger style from Scruggs. Soon the Stanley band was playing the modern bluegrass of Flatt and Scruggs, and Bristol could boast of two of the first three real bluegrass bands. Thus Bristol, the city where Jimmie Rodgers and the Carter Family had made their first records some twenty years before, hosted another historic music development in 1948.

Radio was the prime medium for early bluegrass, but not the only one. The major record companies were rather slow to record bluegrass, and in 1946 Tennessee saw the start of the phenomenon of the independent regional company. This first regional label was Rich-R-Tone, founded by Johnson City businessman Jim Stanton. Starting on a shoestring, Stanton's company soon grew in prestige and popularity, and a number of influential bluegrass groups started with it: the Stanley Brothers, the Bailey Brothers, the Church Brothers, James and Martha Carson, and Wilma Lee and Stoney Cooper. Because he was located in northeastern Tennessee, Stanton was able to attract

Jim Stanton, the Johnson City businessman who founded an early Tennessee regional label, Rich-R-Tone, in 1946, is shown here with two of the singing stars he recorded, the Bailey Brothers. In these 1947 appearances, Danny and Charles Bailey (in light suits) join Stanton (dark suit) in a publicity pose and in hawking records inside a store.

performers from the Carolinas, Virginia, West Virginia, and Kentucky, as well as Tennessee. In a sense, Stanton was documenting the radio music of the area, since most of his artists were basically local radio performers. In fact, Stanton did most of his recording in radio stations of the area. He himself handled most of the distribution and promotion. He recalled:

> In the beginning I would hit the road, fill the car all full of records, and peddle records. I had an Oldsmobile, I believe it was a '39 or '40 model— big gas-drinking four-door monster. Stores got used to this type of delivery and they'd say, "You got this one in the car? You got this in the car?" And I'd take out of the car what I had, and what I didn't we'd write orders and ship.

Yet this kind of approach worked, simply because the customers realized that Rich-R-Tone had their kind of music. In a sense, Stanton's approach marked a return to the technique used by the companies to market old-time music in the 1920s: in both cases, the records were designed for a limited and specific audience, and this helped maintain sales as well as preserve the music's character. The difference—and it was a big one—was that Stanton's was a genuine grass-roots operation. Bluegrass historian Pete Kuykendall has written that Rich-R-Tone was "one of the few commercial record companies which released folk music or songs without the intent or purpose of releasing 'Folk Music.' This type was THE music in that area." In this sense, Rich-R-Tone was a real pioneering label: it was probably the first independent country label devoted to traditional music forms and originating in the same area as the music.

It was in this milieu that the music of Flatt and Scruggs flourished, and they achieved their first success on their own. By 1949 they were becoming well known as recording stars. Monroe, for his part, continued to maintain a band that became a school for many excellent bluegrass musicians. Though Monroe stayed on at the Opry, the main thrust of bluegrass music remained in East Tennessee, in Virginia, and in North Carolina. Through the 1950s and 1960s, second and even third generations of bluegrass pickers carried the music even further. For a time the Chattanooga area became a center for what was to be called "newgrass," and performers like Walter Forbes and Norman Blake attracted national attention with their innovative playing. In the 1960s, northern audiences discovered bluegrass during the folk revival, and soon Flatt and Scruggs found themselves being asked to play universities and northern concert halls. In 1964 they played their famous "Foggy Mountain Breakdown" in Carnegie Hall. Without making any compromises to modern commercial pop music, the bluegrass pickers had achieved the same pinnacle of respectability occupied by Eddy Arnold.

5. Nashville Skyline

As the music developed into the late 1940s, the name *hillbilly* was used less and less, and the new name *country and western* became common. Furthermore, the change was not made so much from outside the music as from inside. To a great extent the change was initiated by the music colony developing in Nashville. John D. Loudermilk, a song writer who settled in Nashville in 1959, reflected a typical attitude when he said, ''The only way we'll get people to recognize our music is to destroy the stereotype of the hillbilly. . . .'' That Nashville was becoming aware of its music's image and that the music industry in Nashville had indeed the power to alter this image suggest the extent to which the town and its music were dominating the field through the 1950s and 1960s. In the era 1955–1976, thousands of musicians from all over the country flocked to Nashville to record, broadcast, and write songs. Many of these people stayed in Nashville and settled into what became a permanent music colony. It was a colony with a diverse and even cosmopolitan character, and it was soon exercising considerable power not only over country music but also over mainstream pop music as well. It is significant that, by the end of this era, some on Nashville's Music Row were advocating yet another name change, from *country* to *American* music; *country*, like *hillbilly*, had acquired connotations which restricted the music. And much of what happened in Nashville during 1955–1976 ran counter to any definitions which limited country music.

The development of the Nashville recording industry actually began in the 1940s. Victor had recorded unsuccessfully in the city as early as 1928, but most of the recording since then had been in the form of radio transcriptions. These transcriptions were the prototypes of modern LP records and were used widely in the 1930s and 1940s to duplicate as much as thirty minutes of a radio show. Because WSM had by this time (early 1940s) established itself as a major source for network programs, the station's engineers had acquired considerable skill at recording techniques. It was thus natural that about 1945 three WSM engineers—Aaron Shelton, George Reynolds, and Carl Jenkins—

decided to open their own recording studio. They called it Castle Studio because WSM's nickname was "the Air Castle of the South." The "studio" was actually a former dining room in Nashville's old Tulane Hotel, and the three men planned to run it on a part-time basis, moonlighting from their regular chores at WSM. Shelton recalls that they opened the studio because "with the pool of talent gathering here, it would be a natural. We knew it would be easier and much less expensive for one artists-and-repertoire man to come here to record the talent than it would be to take the talent to New York or Chicago."

Actually, the A & R men had already decided this. Paul Cohen, in charge of Decca's country music, was one of the first to sense the potential of recording in Nashville. Cohen supervised the first postwar session by a major company in Nashville in March or April 1945, when he recorded four sides with Red Foley in WSM's Studio B. Cohen later used Castle Studio to record important Opry stars like Ernest Tubb and Kitty Wells. In fact, Shelton and his partners soon found their business so heavy that they began persuading other WSM engineers to help them out. WSM, at first unsure how to react to this moonlighting, finally decided that the Opry came first, that the Opry would not diversify into other areas, and began to discourage such part-time endeavors. In the early 1950s Castle closed, and the three partners went back to work full time at WSM.

However, the trend was set. In 1946 A & R pioneer Steve Scholes recorded in Nashville for RCA Victor, using a site at Fourth and Union Streets that had once been the law office of Andrew Jackson. For a time Scholes shared the studio with the Presbyterian church, but a couple of years later Victor became the first label to have its own studio and permanent A & R men in Nashville. In 1950 Capitol Records became the first major company to locate its director for country music in Nashville, and Mercury Records followed suit in 1952. A number of hit records were recorded in the old Ryman Auditorium, which had become the home of the Opry in the early 1940s. (In fact, a number of non-country pop artists were recorded at the Ryman, including big band leaders Woody Herman and Ray Anthony; even this early in its recording history Nashville was producing pop as well as country music.) Songwriter Fred Rose had a small studio in his own home that produced several hit records, and in 1951 guitar player Chet Atkins convinced RCA Victor that they

These four producers contributed greatly to the emergence of Nashville as a recording center. At top are Paul Cohen (left) and Steve Scholes; below are Fred Rose (left, in a pose dating from his days as a performer in the 1930s) and Owen Bradley.

could convert an old garage into a studio. By the early 1950s, tape recorders had replaced the clumsy lacquer discs that had been used in recording since the 1920s, and this made it possible to make more "perfect" recordings. It was easier to record a song over if mistakes were heard in the first take. Glenn Snoddy, today a local studio executive, recalls working on an early Johnnie and Jack session where they did some nineteen takes of a song called "Jesus Hits Like an Atom Bomb"; it was "enough to send me scurrying for the aspirin bottle!" But in spite of these excesses, by the late 1950s the new studios were working overtime, and some were being used up to twenty-four hours a day.

As the major labels were deciding to record their country music in Nashville, the city was also producing a number of independent home-grown labels. The first of the successful Nashville independents was Bullet Records, founded in the mid-1940s by Jim Bulleit. Bullet recorded in Nashville as well as in other cities and was the first label to distribute its product nationally out of Nashville. Yet the Bullet catalog was by no means exclusively country: the first big hit was a popular song called "Near You" performed by the orchestra of Francis Craig, a bandleader who had played on WSM since its opening night. Other Bullet artists ranged from western swing star Johnnie Lee Wills to blues pianist Cecil Gant to folksinger Bradley Kincaid to guitarist Chet Atkins. Other independent labels starting up in Nashville in the late 1940s and early 1950s reflected this same mixture of pop, blues, and country. These labels included Tennessee/Republic, Speed, J–B, Nashboro, Dixie Jamboree, Hillbilly All Star, World, Gold, Excello, Hickory, and Castle. Many of these independent labels pioneered techniques of promotion and distribution, and helped pave the way for the modern recording industry. That many of these labels also recorded a great deal of early rock (then called "rhythm and blues") by black artists reflects the fact that, by the early 1950s, Nashville was also becoming a blues center of sorts. Radio station WLAC became famous for its all-night "soul music" programs, and under the direction of men like Hoss Allen the station soon became an informal center for local black jazz and blues musicians. The city soon saw its first integrated recording session, which was apparently a Cecil Gant session sponsored by Bullet.

Although the major record companies were sending more and more of their executives to work with the growing Nashville recording scene, two native Tennesseans were really the most responsible for what was soon to be called "the Nashville sound." These men were Owen Bradley and Chet Atkins; they, more than anyone else, helped create the special qualities that made a Nashville recording different from others and made a Nashville recording session a unique blend of creativity and technology.

Owen Bradley spent most of his early career as a musician and arranger. Born in Westmoreland, Tennessee, in 1915, he played guitar, piano, harmonica, and vibes and for a time played with the famous dance band of Ted Weems. Bradley, musical director of WSM radio by the late 1940s, was working as an assistant to Paul Cohen, Decca's country A & R man. Bradley was by nature an informal and easygoing man who spoke with a rural flavor and shunned neckties. He was fascinated with the developing recording technology and learned much from Cohen's early recordings on location in Nashville. In 1952 Bradley opened a little film studio in downtown Nashville where he produced short documentary films; soon, however, he was moonlighting in his own film studio by recording in it singers like Ernest Tubb and Kitty Wells. Bradley became interested in using varying amounts of echo in his records, and this led him to build another studio on Sixteenth Avenue South in Nashville; this studio was in the basement of an old house and was one of the earliest music establishments on the street that was later to become known as "Music Row." Here Bradley recorded a number of the new stars emerging in the 1950s, including Marty Robbins, Johnny Cash, Sonny James, and Ferlin Husky. Next to the old house was a quonset hut which Bradley was using for his filmmaking. About 1955 Bradley flew to New York and purchased a new three-track stereo console to install in his quonset hut. The new studio soon became known simply as The Quonset Hut, and it proved to have superb acoustics. Bradley created an echo chamber and devised new ways to record drums, which were becoming more frequently used in country music. The facility soon became recognized as Nashville's finest, and in 1962 Bradley was persuaded to sell it to Columbia Records for over $300,000. Columbia built its entire complex *around* the Quonset Hut, not daring to touch it or interfere with its unique sound. Bradley's contract with Columbia had forbidden him to build another studio in Davidson County (surrounding Nashville) for five years, but in 1965 Bradley found an old barn in neighboring Wilson County (about twenty miles from downtown Nashville) and decided to convert it to a studio. The informal country atmosphere appealed to Nashville musicians, and the sound soon became as legendary as that of the Quonset Hut. Bradley's Barn (as the new studio soon was called) was being booked fourteen to fifteen hours a day. It is hard to say which appealed more: Bradley's technical know-how or the informal atmosphere at his sessions. But recording executive Glenn Snoddy remarks: "If we are to pass out bouquets, a floral arrangement would be due this man for his efforts in establishing the Nashville Sound." And Bradley himself defined the Nashville Sound to writer Paul Hemphill this way: "It isn't so much a sound as it is a way of doing things. It's a bunch of good musicians getting together and doing what comes

PRODUCED BY BULLET RECORDING & TRANSCRIPTION CO.—NASHVILLE, TENN.

Bullet
ALWAYS A SMASH HIT

Vocal
by Bob Lamm

1001 B

NEAk YOU
(Craig-Goell)

Francis Craig and His Orchestra
Francis Craig at the Piano

ONLY FOR THE NON COMMERCIAL USE ON PHONOGRAPHS IN HOMES. MFR. & ORIGINAL PURCHASE OF THIS RECORD SHALL NOT BE RESOLD OR USED FOR ANY OTHER PURPOSE.

EXCELLO
Records

NASHBORO RECORD CO. 177-3RD AVENUE, N. NASHVILLE, TENNESSEE

Excellorec
Music
BMI

Rhythm-Blues
Time 3:05
(a)

MY HOME IS A PRISON
(J. Miller)

Lonesome Sundown

2102

REPUBLIC

Vocal Duet:
Connie and Babe
Oakwood Music

7090
(E4-KB-842)

ROLL ON BLUES
(Gately)

CONNIE AND BABE
and The Black Mountain Boys

REPUBLIC RECORDING CO. • NASHVILLE, TENN.

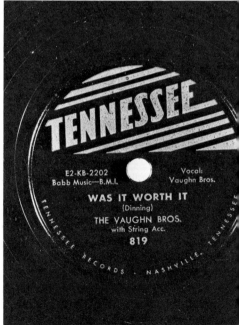

TENNESSEE

E2-KB-2202
Babb Music—B.M.I.

Vocal:
Vaughn Bros.

WAS IT WORTH IT
(Dinning)

THE VAUGHN BROS.
with String Acc.

819

TENNESSEE RECORDS • NASHVILLE, TENNESSEE

naturally. Of course, you've got to have a referee.'' This informal atmosphere of musicians sitting around working out on-the-spot arrangements "by ear" without tension or pressure is what has come to typify recording in Nashville. In pop music, "professionalism" refers to the ability to read music well and perform mechanically under pressure; in Nashville, "professionalism" means the ability to improvise well and perform creatively on demand. Owen Bradley helped legitimize this new style of professionalism.

Chet Atkins was more of a musician than Bradley and made his mark on Nashville both through his music and through his influence as a record producer. Coming from a background of poverty in East Tennessee (born in Luttrell, 1924), Atkins started his career as a fiddler on Knoxville radio and later switched to guitar. For ten years he worked as a sideman for various groups, and in 1950 he landed in Nashville with a Carter Family act. As a skillful and adaptable guitarist, Atkins was soon doing session work for a number of country singers in addition to playing on the Opry. (He played on one of Hank Williams' last sessions and even helped Hank "knock out" a couple of songs.) He also began helping RCA Victor organize sessions—choosing sidemen, suggesting arrangements in the studio—and he did a lot to persuade Victor to set up a studio in Nashville. By 1957 he was in charge of Victor's operation in Nashville and was producing sessions for major country singers. Atkins as a performer was at home in any sort of music, from jazz to pop to classical guitar; "I use parts of everything I've ever heard in my music," he says. This broadmindedness allowed him to modernize and popularize many of the country records he produced. Most people agree today that it was Atkins who, in the late 1950s and early 1960s, "took country music uptown." His records for Victor were even more toward the direction of easy listening and pop music than were Eddy Arnold's and Ernie Ford's. Atkins may not have started each innovation, but he was quick to develop its potential. These innovations included the use of overdubbing in recordings; the use of vocal group backing of a singer; the removal of the heretofore obligatory steel guitar and fiddle, and the introduction of horns and strings; and the elevation of the piano to a major instrument, especially when played in the "slip-note" style of Floyd Cramer. Atkins, one of the few liberals in Nashville's music community, also pioneered in his signing of Charley Pride, the first major black country singer. And unlike many Nashville musicians, Atkins did not try to ignore the rock revolution of the 1950s: he personally

A selection of Nashville's independent record labels of the late 40s and early 50s shows that the productions were varied, ranging from big band hits ("Near You") to blues ("My Home is a Prison") to bluegrass (by Connie and Babe and by the Vaughan Brothers).

played on some of Elvis Presley's sessions, as well as sessions by the Everly Brothers. Atkins too has been called a father of the "Nashville Sound," but, like Owen Bradley, he says there is no technical definition of the sound: "It is the musicians. Southern people have a relaxed way of life, a relaxed way of playing." But Atkins recognized his influence in modernizing country music and later came to have qualms about it. In 1976 he told *Rolling Stone*: "I've said that I hope country music doesn't completely lose its identity—and I apologized for anything I did in taking it too far uptown, which I sometimes did because we were just trying to sell records."

Many people, awed by Atkins' success as a producer, overlook the other way he has affected country music: through his guitar style. Atkins plays a "Travis style" fingerpicking learned from Kentucky guitarist Merle Travis. Atkins' style utilizes the thumb for bass and rhythm and three fingers for the melody (though Travis used thumb and one finger). The style, also called "western Kentucky choking style," originated even before Travis with older black Kentucky guitarists like Jim Mason and Arnold Schultz, who probably based the style on even earlier folk traditions. But Atkins recorded the style far more than did Travis: from the early 1950s Atkins made over forty LP albums for Victor. Many contained country songs picked in Atkins' style, but others featured pop songs performed in the same style. Though these albums were not national best-sellers, they influenced generations of pickers throughout the South. They also helped popularize the notion that "crossover" could flow both ways: that country could be defined as style as much as content, and that a pop song could sound country when fingerpicked à la Atkins. Atkins' performances with the Boston Pops Orchestra and at the Newport Jazz Festival also helped win recognition of the guitar as a serious solo instrument.

As the recording industry grew in Nashville, so did the important "support" industry of music publishing. By 1950 sheet music publication was no longer a major source of income to song writers or singers, but publication was nonetheless necessary to secure copyrights and assure the song writer of royalties from performances of his material. It was becoming possible for country song writing to become a full-time profession—an important new development. Historically country music song writers had performed their own material and made their living primarily as performers. (One of the few exceptions was Memphis-born Bob Miller, who wrote hundreds of songs in the 1920s and 1930s and saw them recorded by pioneers like Vernon Dalhart, but Miller was able to do this only because he was located in New York and was able to work through the structure already established in Tin Pan Alley.) Acuff-Rose, the first Nashville-based publisher, was formed in 1942 by singer

Roy Acuff and pop song writer Fred Rose. Acuff was getting suspicious because New York publishers were offering so much for his songs and decided to protect himself. Acuff-Rose enjoyed its first national hit with "Tennessee Waltz" in 1950 and remains today one of the most prestigious Nashville publishers. It was the first Nashville publisher to receive pop music awards, the first to have its own recording studio, and the first to expand to international operation. Acuff-Rose was followed in 1953 by Jim Denny's Cedarwood Publishing Company and in 1954 by Tree Publishing Company. By 1959 Opry star Marty Robbins, who had written successfully for Acuff-Rose, set a trend by establishing his own publishing firm. By 1960 the city could claim about 100 such publishers, and in 1975 this figure had grown to 244. Many were tiny publishers with only one or two hit songs to their credit; others were dominated by one performing star; and still others were large operations geared to the new class of professional song writers and modeled on the Tin Pan Alley operations of New York. A further sign of Nashville's new importance to publishing was the location there of branches of the country's three music licensing corporations. These organizations act as clearing houses for performing rights: anyone performing songs on radio or TV or in concerts and clubs has to pay a royalty or fee to the licensing corporation, which in turn distributes the money to the proper writers and publishers. Broadcast Music Incorporated (BMI), the first of the organizations to recognize country song writers, opened a Nashville office in 1958; the other two, ASCAP (American Society of Composers, Authors, and Publishers) and SESAC (Selected Editions of Standard American Catalogues), followed suit in the early 1960s.

But in spite of the new methods of recording and song publishing, most professional country singers still made most of their money from personal appearances. *Billboard* magazine, the leading trade journal of the music industry, has described personal appearances as "the bread-and-butter department for countless country artists, bookers and promoters." These personal appearances took all forms, from state fairs to night clubs, but since about 1950 the most common form of country show has been the "onenighter" or "auditorium show," where several singers would combine their talents in a show staged in a large arena seating one thousand or more people. Nashville had been a center for talent booking since the early 1930s, when the Opry formed its own talent agency. Yet many performers still did their own booking, and as late as the early 1950s much booking in Nashville was still done through the switchboard operator at the Opry. In 1954 Jim Denny, WSM's Artists' Service Bureau manager, left WSM to start his own talent agency and set the stage for other independent agencies to follow. By 1966

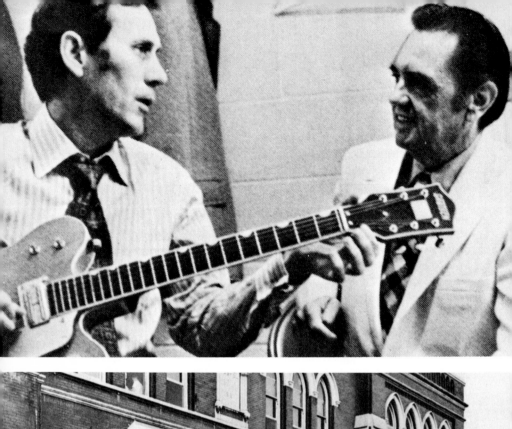

there were twelve major talent agencies in the city, and in 1975 there were sixty-five (though by this time some were dealing with non-country entertainment).

During all this the music continued to develop. The Opry roster grew until it numbered more than 150, and the diversity of the new acts to some extent reflected the changing times, the expanded definition of country music, and the emerging "Nashville Sound." To be sure, new acts reflected the older traditions of the music: the Louvin Brothers and Wilma Lee and Stoney Cooper represented the vocal harmonies of the 1930s, Hank Snow carried on the Jimmie Rodgers style, and the bluegrass genre was represented by fiddler Benny Martin, Flatt and Scruggs (returning as a separate act), Jim and Jesse McReynolds, and the Osborne Brothers. In the classic honky-tonk tradition were singers such as Porter Wagoner, Stonewall Jackson, and George Jones, and the new crooner tradition was carried on by men like George Hamilton IV and Bill Anderson. Other country music forms also found their way onto the Opry stage: the Cajun tradition of Jimmy C. Newman, the ragtime piano of Del Wood, the rustic humor of Archie Campbell, or the pop cowboy songs of Marty Robbins.

By this time women had come into their own as country stars. Although several women such as Maybelle and Sara Carter, Patsy Montana, and Lula Belle had been important pioneers in the music, almost inevitably they had been members of groups or duos. Nashville native Kitty Wells (she took her stage name from the old folk song "Dad" Pickard used to sing on the Opry) joined the Opry in 1952 and became its first widely successful solo woman singer. She was soon followed by pop-gospel singer Martha Carson (1952), Jean Shepherd (1955), Skeeter Davis (1959), Dottie West (1964), Connie Smith and Norma Jean (1965), and later Dolly Parton, Loretta Lynn, and Tammy Wynette. But the woman who became most closely identified with the Opry during this time was Centerville, Tennessee's Sarah Ophelia Colley Cannon, also know as Cousin Minnie Pearl. Although Minnie Pearl sings on her stage shows, mostly she specializes in comedy monologues about the mythical rural community of Grinder's Switch. Her famous costume includes a cotton dress and a big-brimmed hat with the price tag hanging on it. Minnie's creator was actually a graduate from the prestigious Ward-Belmont College in Nashville, and she worked for several years producing amateur plays in the

Guitarist Chet Atkins, pictured here with his mentor Merle Travis, has made major contributions to country music—both on stage and behind the scenes. Below, the old Ryman Auditorium in downtown Nashville was home of the Opry from the end of World War II until 1974.

rural areas of north Georgia. There she hit upon the idea for the Minnie Pearl character and begain using it when she first joined the Opry in 1940. The 1970s saw Minnie as one of the three or four superstars on the Opry, delighting audiences who for some thirty years now have watched her figure out ways to catch a man.

In the mid-1950s another event occurred that was to push Nashville and the Opry even more in the direction of pop music: the rise of rock. During this time, the creative impulse of the music shifted again from Nashville to another section of Tennessee: the Memphis delta. There singers—Elvis Presley, Johnnie Cash, Jerry Lee Lewis, Roy Orbison, and Carl Perkins, for example—were causing Nashville country bookers to look anxiously over their shoulders, and a shoestring record company called Sun Records was causing the major Nashville studios to reassess their philosophy.

The genius behind Sun Records was an Alabama man named Sam Phillips. Phillips opened up a recording service in Memphis in 1950, and two years later turned it into Sun Records. Memphis had always been a center for blues, but since the late 1930s it had been a meeting ground for other types of music, both from east and west. In the late 1930s the city had seen the rise of the Swift Jewel Cowboys, a remarkable country band fusing elements of western swing, ragtime, blues, and country, and in the late 1940s harmonica players Wayne Rainey and Lonnie Glosson injected a blues sound into the country music of the Delmore Brothers. Phillips started out documenting this black blues tradition, and in his first three years he had discovered important modern blues artists like Junior Parker and Ike Turner. In 1955 Phillips began recording country acts; his first was an old minstrel show veteran named Harmonica Frank, but he soon began to experiment with various mixtures of blues and country. One of these was a style formed by adding drums to up-tempo country music, a style that soon evolved into "rockabilly." One of Phillips' first great rockabilly successes was a northwest Tennessee native named Carl Perkins; Perkins started recording for Sun in the Hank Williams style, but in 1956 moved toward rockabilly and had a national hit with a song called "Blue Suede Shoes." Other white Sun artists from the Memphis area, many of whom have dropped into obscurity today, made records which greatly influenced the development of rock.

Phillips had always said that he could make it big if he could find a white singer who sounded like a Negro. He found such a singer in 1954, when he first recorded Elvis Presley. Presley, a native of Tupelo, Mississippi, reflected his willingness to mix country and blues on his first record: one side was an old blues tune, "That's All Right, Mama," backed with Bill Monroe's "Blue Moon of Kentucky." But it was style as much as repertoire that made Presley:

his style was nothing like earlier white blues styles (such as Jimmie Rodgers')
but was characterized by Presley's trembling, emotional voice which at times
seems barely under control. After making only ten records with Presley,
Phillips sensed that his small company could just not handle Presley's immense success. He willingly sold Presley's contract to RCA Victor for $35,000
and soon watched him become an unparalleled national phenomenon.

Phillips used the money from the Presley contract as capital to develop
more country and rockabilly acts. In 1955 he found Arkansas singer Johnny
Cash, who soon had national hits with "Folsom Prison Blues" and "I Walk
the Line." Using a spare, basic country band called "the Tennessee Three,"
Cash sang in a non-nasal baritone that endeared him to thousands of people
who could not stand more conventional country music. He, like Presley, left
Sun after a couple of years, moved to California, and did not reenter the
Tennessee music scene until the late 1960s, when he had become an accepted
superstar. Far more rock-oriented than Cash was yet another Phillips discov-
ery, Louisiana pianist Jerry Lee Lewis. Lewis worked as a session man on
hundreds of Sun sides and then achieved national success as a rock star in the
late 1950s. Through the years, Lewis never cut his country ties, and it is
reflective of the opening up of country music that Lewis today is recognized as
country by the Nashville establishment.

Phillips at first was doing about the same thing in West Tennessee that
Rich-R-Tone's Jim Stanton was doing in East Tennessee: running a small
independent company featuring a rather primitive but vital music and market-
ing it to a regional audience. Both men succeeded in giving Nashville music
sorely needed injections of excitement and purpose. Both acted as middlemen
in bringing to commercial country music still more of the vitality of genuine
folk music. For the new sound from Memphis first frightened and then
intrigued the Nashville crowd, and soon Chet Atkins was producing rock
sessions, and rockabilly acts like the Everly Brothers were regulars on the
Opry. Rockabilly was gone by 1960, absorbed into the mainstream of
Nashville country music. Sam Phillips, who for a time had found himself
running a national label (he shipped most of his Johnny Cash LPs, for
instance, to Minnesota), slipped back to the status of a regional producer, and
he finally phased out Sun in 1968.

Meanwhile the Nashville recording industry kept growing bigger and more
complex. The LP record album was introduced in 1948 and contained the
equivalent of twelve 78-rpm sides; it soon became the basic unit of recording
for most country singers, and before long the phrase "new record" came to
refer to an album of twelve songs instead of two. This created even more of a
demand for song writers, publishers, musicians, and technicians. The wide

Sun Records, the Memphis-based label established by Sam Phillips, had Nashville looking westward for new sounds during the rise of rock in the mid-50s. Elvis Presley's first country-tinged records were issued by Sun in 1954—this one with Scotty Moore, guitar, and Bill Black, bass.

use of stereo tape in the 1960s meant even more technology and even more behind-the-scenes men. Musicians' unions grew, and country music became big business. By the early 1970s, Nashville's music industry included over 1,000 musicians, 900 song writers, over 30 recording studios, 90 record companies, 244 music publishers, 10 record-pressing plants, and 11 television program production companies, and the industry was pumping about $100 million yearly into Nashville's economy. To train new people for this new and complex business, two area colleges in the early 1970s devised college programs leading to degrees in recording industry management.

This growth was only partly due to the increasing nationwide acceptance of country music records. Many popular and rock singers were coming to Nashville to take advantage of the advanced technology, informal recording methods, and excellent sidemen. A familiar remark among record executives of the 1960s was: "Nashville is a musical Mayo Clinic for ailing acts. The pop singer takes the Nashville treatment and either recovers or dies." By 1966 *Newsweek* was reporting that "nearly one out of every two pop records in America" was made in Nashville. Nashville's studios received even more recognition in 1969 when folk-rock star Bob Dylan recorded there; within a few years former Beatles Ringo Starr and Paul McCartney were recording in Nashville and using Nashville sidemen. One British rock group was so impressed with its recording facilities that they named their entire album "Bradley's Barn."

Country music continued to attract more and more visitors to Nashville, though in different ways and through different media. The original Nashville appeal was basically a sound, using only auditory media of radio and records. For some time the Opry clung to this approach; the National Life Company was hesitant to exploit the Opry's success in areas other than radio, for they felt they had expertise in radio and none in other media. But for some years the Opry had had an important visual dimension: the performers wore flashy sequined suits (or wild comedy outfits), Roy Acuff did yo-yo tricks, and two or three times a night square dancers took the stage. This visual dimension of the show was, of course, lost on the radio audience but appealed to the 3,500 people in the live audience. As network radio declined, and radio in general declined in the face of television, farsighted producers could see the time when the Opry would have more importance as a live event than as a radio show. An increasing tourist trade was coming into Nashville, lured by the Opry, by tours of stars' homes, and by the recently built Country Music Hall of Fame. It was an awareness of this tourist potential that finally led National Life to "merchandise" the Opry. In 1972 the company opened Opryland, a giant amusement park built around a new, multimillion-dollar Opry house. The park, which attracts far more people than can get in to see the Opry, features all types of American pop music in addition to country; it reflects, to some extent, the general movement in Nashville toward "mainstream" American music.

The town also became a center for television production. It was not wishful thinking that prompted WSM to install in their new Opry house a sophisticated television studio. During the decade 1966–1975 a number of major national network shows originated individual programs from Nashville, and several popular country music series were completely produced in Nashville. The Opry itself had been through several network TV stints in the late 1950s and

early 1960s; in the end it was the individual Opry stars who succeeded in television. In 1969 Johnny Cash had a regular network program that was partly broadcast out of a couple of trailers parked in back of the old Ryman Auditorium. In that same year CBS initiated a zany country comedy-and-music show, "Hee Haw," which was produced in a downtown Nashville TV studio. But most television series from Nashville have been produced and distributed on a syndicated basis: the series are not sold to a major network but directly to the individual broadcasting stations around the country. This method, which has been called "grass roots TV," has produced shows by singers like Bill Anderson, the Willis Brothers, Porter Wagoner, Jimmy Dean, and Dolly Parton, as well as anthology shows like "Pop Goes the Country," "Nashville on the Road," "That Good Ole Nashville Music," and a revived version of "Hee Haw."

And in 1975 the town was the subject of a major American film, *Nashville*. Directed by Robert Altman, one of the country's most respected filmmakers, *Nashville* reflected the country's recognition of Nashville's new status as a major cultural symbol. In fact, Altman later admitted that he saw the town, with its music and mystique, as functioning as a modern Hollywood.

All of which brings us back to the most basic of questions: why Nashville? Why did the country music and the recording industry and the "dream factory" develop here? One immediate cause was the presence of the Grand Ole Opry and the willingness of National Life and WSM to sustain the Opry through good times and hard times. The Opry was originally sustained as a means to sell products to a certain geographic or economic group of people, and somewhere along the line it became the product itself. WSM and the Opry acted as a training school for many of the important figures in the Nashville recording industry: Opry or WSM veterans helped establish the first publishing house, the first recording studio, and the first major talent agency, and they were in key positions with record companies. The Opry also attracted the pool of talent that lured the recording industry to the town. The Opry was not the only country radio show of note, but it grew more because of Nashville's central location in the South and because it was near the fans of country music, thus facilitating tours and personal appearances so necessary to keep performers alive in the early days of professionalism. Nashville, too, represented a meeting ground between the authentic folk roots of country music and the

Nashville's prominent Woodland studio (its control room shown above) is where a rock group, the Nitty Gritty Dirt Band, made history in 1971 when it recorded an album featuring such stars as those below: from left, Roy Acuff, Jimmy Martin, Mother Maybelle Carter, and Doc Watson.

technology necessary to commercialize it. The hills and hollows of Tennessee constantly produced a steady stream of native musical talent which constantly rejuvenated and reinforced the music. As late as 1972, when country music had certainly ceased to be a regional phenomenon, the prestigious *Country Music Who's Who* listed forty-four major country stars as coming from Tennessee—more than any other state except Texas. And, as we have seen, many of the important behind-the-scenes people in the music, from Chet Atkins to Owen Bradley to Jim Denny, have been native Tennesseans.

In more recent years, Tennessee has been active in recognizing and preserving this heritage. Country music has been recognized as a serious cultural development worthy of academic study, and a major resource and history library, the Country Music Foundation, has been established in Nashville. Grand Ole Opry stars have appeared in formal concerts at the Smithsonian Institution in Washington. The folk music traditions of Tennessee have been documented and preserved by statewide organizations such as the Tennessee Folklore Society, founded in 1934 and active today. Folk music from the Memphis delta is being preserved by more recent organizations like the Center for Southern Folklore, while Appalachian music is being captured on videotape by an innovative young organization called Broadside TV. In 1975 Tennessee appointed an official state folklorist, one of the first states to do so. Some old-time fiddling fans banded together in 1967 to form the Tennessee Valley Old Time Fiddlers' Association, an organization which has remained active in sponsoring and regulating fiddling contests in Tennessee, Kentucky, and Alabama. Even the Grand Ole Opry recognized the importance of old-time fiddling when it initiated one of the country's most challenging invitational fiddling contests, the Grand Masters, in the early 1970s. Indeed, today the residents of Tennessee seem more appreciative than ever of their native folk music heritage; in 1975 over fifteen major folk festivals were scheduled in the state, and this does not include dozens of smaller festivals held at shopping centers and county fairs. Audiences seem to exist for both the polished, uptown "Nashville Sound" and the simple, lonesome sound of the mountain fiddle—and it is characteristic of Tennessee that in many cases it is one and the same audience.

Traditional music today thrives in Tennessee side by side with the Nashville sound. At gatherings such as the annual state championship fiddling contest in Clarksville, one can still see everything from buck dancing to spoon playing.

Selected Resources on Country Music

An author's resources invariably include advice and information from knowledgeable friends and colleagues. Especially helpful in this instance were Dick Hulan, Steve Davis, Bill Harrison, Linnell Gentry, Ken Irwin, Marian Leighton, Bob Taylor, Ralph Hyde, and the staff of the Country Music Foundation. In addition, my research was assisted by the Middle Tennessee State University Faculty Research Fund, for which I am grateful. Further information about Tennessee folk music can be found in the specific books and articles listed below, as well as in such publications as *Old Time Music*, *JEMF Quarterly*, *The Journal of Country Music*, *Bluegrass Unlimited*, *The Devil's Box*, *Pickin'*, and *Country Music*.

Atkins, Chet, with Bill Neely. *Country Gentleman*. New York: Ballantine, 1975.
Boswell, George. "Progress Report: Collection of Tennessee Folksongs in Recent Years." *Tennessee Folklore Society Bulletin* XXV (June 1959), 31–79.
Ford, Ira. *Traditional Music of America*. 2d ed. Hatsboro, Pa.: Folklore Associates, 1965.
Gentry, Linnell. *A History and Encyclopedia of Country, Western, and Gospel Music*. 2d ed. Nashville: Clairmont Corp., 1969.
Green, Archie. *Only a Miner. Studies in Recorded Coal-Mining Songs*. Urbana: Univ. of Illinois Press, 1972.
Green, Douglas B. *Country Roots. The Origins of Country Music*. New York: Hawthorn, 1976.
Hemphill, Paul. *The Nashville Sound: Bright Lights and Country Music*. New York: Simon and Schuster, 1970.
Hurst, Jack. *Nashville's Grand Ole Opry*. New York: Abrams, 1975.
Jackson, George Pullen. *White Spirituals in the Southern Uplands*. Chapel Hill: Univ. of North Carolina Press, 1933.

Kirkland, Edwin C. "Check List of the Titles of Tennessee Folksongs."
     Journal of American Folklore LIX (1946), 423–76.
Laws, G. Malcolm. *Native American Balladry*. Philadelphia: AFS Bibliog-
     raphical and Special Series, Vol. 1, 1950.
Malone, Bill C. *Country Music, U.S.A.: A Fifty-Year History*. Austin: Univ.
     of Texas Press, 1968.
————, and Judith McCulloh, eds. *Stars of Country Music: Uncle Dave
     Macon to Johnny Rodriguez*. Urbana: Univ. of Illinois Press, 1975.
Sharp, Cecil. *English Folk Songs from the Southern Appalachians*, ed. Maud
     Karpeles. 2 vols. London and New York: Oxford Univ. Press, 1932.
Shelton, Robert, with Burt Goldblatt. *The Country Music Story*. Rev. ed.
     Secaucus, N.J.: Castle, 1966.
Sturdivant, John, ed. *Country Music Who's Who 1972*. Nashville: Record
     World, 1971.
Wolfe, Charles. "Early Country Music in Knoxville." *Old Time Music*, No.
     10 (Spring 1974), 19–31.
————. *Grand Ole Opry: The Early Years 1925–1935*. London: Old Time
     Music, 1975.
———— "Ralph Peer at Work: The Victor 1927 Bristol Sessions." *Old Time
     Music*, No. 5 (Summer 1972), 10–15.
————, ed. *Truth is Stranger Than Publicity. The Autobiography of Alton
     Delmore*. Nashville: Country Music Foundation Press, 1977.

Index

(References to illustrations are in bold type)

Acuff, Roy, 8, 25, 30, 36, 48, 59, **71**, 72–75, 80, 86, 101, 107–**108**
Acuff-Rose publishing company, 81, 100–101
Aeolian-Vocalion Company, 28, 32, **34**, 35
AFRS transcriptions, 75
Allen Brothers, 49–50
Allen, Hoss, 96
Altman, Robert, 109
American Record Company, 73
"Amos n' Andy" (radio show), 64
Anderson, Bill, 103, 109
Anglin, Jack, 86
Anthony, Ray, 94
Armstrong, Shed, 20, **21**
Arnold, Eddy, 76, 78, **79**–80, 82, 92, 99
Arrington, Charlie, **68**–69
Artists' Service Bureau (WSM), 64, 69
ASCAP, 101
Ashley, Tom, **39**, 47
Atkins, Chet, 86, **87**, 94, 96, 99–100, **102**, 105, 111
Austin, Gene, 32
Ayers, Harry, 50

Bailey Brothers, 88, **91**
Bailey, Deford, 60, 63, 64, **65**
Ballet cards, 7, 8, **9**
"Barn Dance" (WSM), 59, 61
"Barrel of Fun" (WJHC), 88, 90
Bascom, Louise Rand, 19, 22
Bate, Alcyone, 59, **68**, 69
Bate, Buster, **68**, 69
Bate, Dr. Humphrey, 55, 59, 60, 61, **62**, 63, **68**, 69
Bennett, Tony, 78
Berle, Milton, 80
Binkley Brothers' Dixie Clodhoppers, 61

Binkley Brothers' String Orchestra, 61
Black, Bill, 106
Blake, Norman, 92
Blanchard, Lowell, 85–86
Bluegrass, 82–92, 103
Blues, 10, 50, 52, 63, 67, 84, 96, 104, 105
Blue Sky Boys, 48
BMI, 101
"Boone County Jamboree" (WLW), 48
Boston Pops Orchestra, 100
Boswell, George, 6, 7, 20
Bowman, Charlie, 41–42, **45**, 90
Bowman Sisters, 41
Bradley, Owen, **95**, 96–99, 100, 107, 111
Brewster, Brothers, 88
Broadside ballad, 7
Broadside TV, 111
Brown, Henry, **87**
Bryan, William Jennings, 10
Buckwheat notes, 12
Bulleit, Jim, 96
Bullet Records, 96, **98**
Burnett, Dick, 8, 9
Burns, Jethro, 86
Butler, Carl, 77

Camel Caravan, 75
Campbell, Archie, 86, 103
Cannon, Ophelia Colley. *See* Minnie Pearl
Capitol Records, 94
Carlisle, Bill, 86
Carolina Tar Heels, 47
Carson, James and Martha, 90, 103
Carson, Fiddlin' John, 25–28, **31**, **39**, 40, 72
Carter, A. P., 14
Carter Family, 14, 33, 44, 46, 77, 90, 99, 103
Carter, Maybelle, 44, 69, **108**

Cash, Johnny, 97, 104–105, 109
Castle Records, 96
Castle Studio, 94
Cedarwood Publishing Company, 101
Center for Southern Folklore, 111
Child, Francis, 6
Church Brothers, 90
Churchill, Allen, 82
Clements, Zeke, and his Bronco Busters, 70
Coats, Mr. and Mrs. Gabriel, 4–5
Cohen, Paul, 94–**95**, 97
Collins, Floyd, 10, 30
Columbia Records, 28, 97
Columbian Harmony (Moore), 12
Como, Perry, 80
Confrey, Zez, 27
Connie and Babe, 98
Cooper, Wilma Lee and Stoney, 90, 103
Cope Brothers, 88
Country music, naming of, 42, 93
Country Music Foundation, 111
Country Music Hall of Fame, 107
Country Music Who's Who, 111
Craig, Edwin, 54
Craig, Francis, 55, 96
Craig, Percy, 56
Cramer, Floyd, 99
Crook Brothers, 60
Crosby, Bing, 32, 40, 75, 78, 84
Cross, Hugh Ballard, 48
"Crossover hit," 78

Dalhart, Vernon, 100
Davenport, Cal, 49, **87**
Davenport, Homer, 49
Davenport, Hubert, **87**
Darnell, Bob, **87**
Davis, Claude, 50
Davis, Skeeter, 103
Dean, Jimmy, 109
DeArmond, Dr. Dave, 20, **21**
Delmore Brothers, 14, 36, 48, 67, 69, 104
Denny, Jim, 101, 111
Dixie Jamboree Record Company, 96
Dixieliners, 67, 69–**70**. *See also* Sam and Kirk
   McGee, Arthur Smith
Douglas, Bob, 50
Dromgoole, Wil Allen, 23
Dunham, Millie, 58
Dylan, Bob, 30, 107

Easterly, Jess, **71**
Edison, Thomas, 32

Event songs, 7–8
Everly Brothers, 100, 105
Excello Records, 96, **98**

"Farm and Fun Time" (WCYB), 90
"Fasola" singing, 12
"Fiddle and the Bow" (Taylor), 25
Fiddling contests, 19–23, 40, **110**, 111
Field recording, 43
Flatt, Lester, **83**, 84–85, 88, 90, 92, 103
Fleming, Reece, 52
Floyd, Harmonica Frank, 104
Foley, Red, 94
Forbes, Walter, 92
Ford, Henry, 3, 56
Ford, Tennessee Ernie, 78–**79**, 80–81, 88, 99
Forrester, Howdy, 59
Frank, J. L., 75
Fruit Jar Drinkers, 61

Gamble, James, 18
Gant, Cecil, 96
Gapped scale, 10
Glosson, Lonnie, 104
Godfrey, Arthur, 80
Gold Record Company, 96
Goodman, Herald, 66
"The Good Old Way," 12, **13**
Gore, Albert, 25
Grand Masters' Fiddling Contest, 111
"Grand Ole Opry" (WSM), vii, 5–6, 36, 54,
   63, 64, 66, 67, 70–74, 75–76, 81, 84, 86,
   101–104, 107–109, 111
"The Grand Ole Opry," (movie), 74
Grand Ole Opry House, 5, 107–108
Grant, Jack and Claude, 46
Grayson, G. B., **39**, 46–47
Greene, Jack, 77
Griffin, Bartley, 20, **21**
Guitar, early history of, 41
Gully Jumpers, **68**, 69
Guthrie, Woody, 30, 70
"Gypsy Laddie," quoted, 4, 5

Hamilton, George IV, 103
Handy, W. C., 52
Hardison, Roy, **68**, 69
Harkreader, Sid, 34–35
Harp of Columbia, 12
Harris, Dedrick, 40
Hatcher, Dynamite, 73
Hawkins, Erskine, 81
Hay, George, 54–66, **57**, **62**, 73
Haynes, "Homer," 86

"Hee Haw," 109
Hemphill, Paul, 97
Herman, Woody, 94
Hesson, Lou, **68, 69**
Hickory Records, 96
Hill Billies, 40–42, 48
Hillbilly All Star Records, 96
Hill, "Smilin' Eddie," 86, **87**
History of Middle Tennessee (Putnam), 17
Honky-tonk music, 76–77
Hope, Bob, 78, 80
Hopkins, Al, 41, 42
Hopkins, Joe, 41
Howard, Clint, 47
Hughes, Charles Evans, 3
Husky, Ferlin, 97
Hutcherson, Burt, 59, **68, 69**

Irving, Maud, 7

J-B Records, 96
Jackson, Andrew, 94
Jackson, George Pullen, 11
Jackson, Jack, **51**
Jackson, Stonewall, 103
James, Sonny, 97
Jean, Norma, 103
Jenkins, Andrew, 30
Jenkins, Carl, 93–94
"Jiggy" bow (fiddle style), 15
Johnnie and Jack, 86, 96
Jones, George, 103
Jones, Grandpa, 32

Karpeles, Maud, 3–4, 10–11
Kentucky Slim, 86, **87**
Kincaid, Bradley, 96
King, Pee Wee, 70, 75–76, 80–81
Kirby, Oswald, **71**
"Kitty Wells" (song), 7–**9**
Knoxville Harmony (Jackson), 12–**13**
Kuykendall, Pete, 92

LP record album, introduced on market, 105–106
Laws, Malcolm, 6
Lewis, Jerry Lee, 104–105
Library of Congress, 43
Loew's Vaudeville, 34
"Long bow" (fiddle style), 15
Loudermilk, John D., 93
Louvin Brothers, 50, 103
Lowery, Ramblin' Red, 52
Lunn, Robert, 70

Lynn, Loretta, 103

Mac and Bob. *See* McFarland and Gardner
Macon, Dorris, **68,** 69
Macon, Uncle Dave, 28, 32–40, **37, 45,** 55, 59, 61, 63–64, 66, **68,** 69, 72, 74
Malone, Bill, 81
Martin, Benny, 103
Martin, Jimmy, **108**
Mason, Jim, 100
McCarroll, Jimmy, 49
McCartney, Paul, 107
McCartt Brothers, 49
McCoy, Charlie, 60
McFarland and Gardner, 48
McGee Brothers, 69
McGee, Kirk, 14, 35, **68–71**
McGee, Sam, 18, 36, **37, 68–71**
McReynolds, Jim and Jesse, 103
Medicine show, 72
Melton, Charley, 60
Memphis Jug Band, 52
Mercury Records, 94
"Mid-Day Merry-Go-Round" (WNOX), 86
Miller, Bob, 100
Miller, "Lost John," 84
Minnie Pearl, 76, **79,** 103–104
Monroe, Bill, 36, 48, 81–82, **83,** 84, 88, 92, 104
Monroe, Birch, **83**
Monroe, Charlie, 47, 48, 84
Montana, Patsy, 103
Moore, Byrd and his Hot Shots, 47
Moore, Scotty, 106
Moore, William, 12
Murphy, Frank "Squire," 48
Music publishing industry, growth of in Nashville, 100–101
Music Row, growth of, 97, 106–107

Nashboro Records, 96
Nashville (film), 109
"Nashville on the Road," 109
"Nashville sound," 103, 111
National Life and Accident Insurance Company, 54–55, 59, 109
NBC, 64
New Harp of Columbia (Swan), 14
Newman, Jimmy C., 103
Newport Jazz Festival, 100
Nitty Gritty Dirt Band, 108

Oaks, Charlie, 7, 10, 28, 30, 32, 41, 48
Okeh Records, 27–28

Old Cabin Music (Nashville), 66
"Old Harp Singers," 14, 47
Opryland (Nashville), 81, 107
Orbison, Roy, 104
Osborne Brothers, 88, 103
Owens, Texas Ruby, 70

Page, Patti, 81
Parker, Colonel Tom, 80
Parker, Junior, 104
Parton, Dolly, 103, 109
Paton, Sandy, 10
Patterson, Andy, 49
Payne, Tom Cat, 50
Peer, Ralph, 44, **45,** 46
Pellettieri, Vito, 64
Perkins, Carl, 104
Perry County Music Makers, 52
Phillips,Sam, 104–105
Pickard Family, 63
Pickard, Obed "Dad," 63, 66, 103
"Pop Goes the Country," 109
Possum Hunters, 59, 61
Poulton, Curt, 66
Presley, Elvis, 80, 100, 104–105, 106
Price, Fred, 47
Pride, Charley, 99
Puckett, Riley, 48
Putnam, A. W., 17
Powers, Fiddlin', 40

Quonset hut (Nashville), 97

Radio stations, start of, 27. *See also* individual
  call letters
Rainey, Wayne, 104
Rann, Grover, 50
RCA Victor, 94, 99, 105. *See also* Victor Com-
  pany
Rector, John, 41
Reneau, George, 28, 30, 32, 33, 48
Reynolds, George, 93–94
Rhythm and blues, 96
Rich-R-Tone records, 90, **91,** 92, 105
Riddle, Jimmy, 60
Ridgel's Fountain Citians, 49
Robbins, Marty, 97, 103
Robinette, Melvin, 53
Rodgers, Jimmie, 40, 44, 46, 52, 76–77, 85,
  90, 103, 105
Roe Brothers, 42, 90
Rolling Stone, 100
Roane County Ramblers, 49
Rose, Fred, 77, 94, **95,** 101

Ryman Auditorium (Nashville), **102,** 109

Sacred Harp, (White and King), 12, 14
Sarie and Sally, 70
"Saturday Night Jamboree" (WOPI), **89**
Scholes, Steve, 94, **95**
Schultz, Arnold, 100
Scruggs, Earl, 40, 49, 82, **83,** 84–85, 88, 90,
  92, 103
"Scruggs, style," 82
Sears Company, 41, 73, 78
Seeger, Mike, 70
Seivers, Fiddlin' Bill, 48–49, **51**
Seivers, Mack, **51**
Seivers, Willie, 49, **51**
Seven shape notes, 14
SESAC, 101
Shape notes, 12, **13,** 52
Sharp, Cecil, 3–4, 5–6, 10–11, 27, 67, 77, 80
Shelton, Aaron, 93–94
Shepherd, Jean, 103
Short Brothers, 81
Shook, Jack and the Missouri Mountaineers, 70
Sinatra, Frank, 75
Singing conventions, 11
Singing master, 11
Singing schools, 11, 25, 47, 52, 67
Sizemore, Asher and Little Jimmie, 66
Skillet Lickers, 48
Smith, Arthur, 69–**71,** 73
Smith, Beasley, 55
Smith, Bessie, 49
Smith, Carl, 76–77
Smith, Connie, 103
Smith, Sawmill, 50
Smith, Slim, 70
Smoky Mountain Boys, **71,** 73
Smoky Mountain Ramblers, 49
Snoddy, Glenn, 96–97
Snow, Hank, 103
Speed Records, 96
Sousa, John Phillip, 60
Southern Moonlight Entertainers, 49
Stanley Brothers, 90
Stanton, Jim, 90, **91,** 92, 105
Starr, Kay, 81
Starr, Ringo, 107
Stephens, Uncle Bunt, 15
Sterchi Brothers Furniture Company, 32, 35,
  47
Stewart, Redd, 81, **83**
Stone, Harry, 64, 73–75
Stone, Oscar, 59
Story, Carl, 90

Stuart, Uncle Am, 28, 30, **31**, 33, **39**, 40, 42, 72
Sun Records, 104–105, **106**
Swan, W. H. and M. L., 14
Swift Jewell Cowboys, 104

Tanner, Gid, 72
Taylor, Alf, 23, **24**, 25
Taylor, Jerry, **51**
Taylor, Jimmy, 23
Taylor, Robert Love, 20, **21**, 22–**24**, 25–28
Temple, Shirley, 66
Tennessee Folklore Society, 111
Tennessee Ramblers, 48, **51**
Tennessee/Republic Records, 96, **98**
Tennessee Valley Old Time Fiddlers' Association, 59, 111
"Tennessee Waltz," as state song, 81–82, 101
Tenneva Ramblers, 46
Thacker, Neb, 49
"That Good Ole Nashville Music," 109
Thompson, Aunt Ella, 58
Thompson, Uncle Jimmy, 19, 56, **57**, 58–59, 61, 63
"To the Fiddlers" (Taylor), 23
Tolbert, "Turtle," 90
Townsend, Respers, 52
Travis, Merle, 81, 100, **102**
Tree Publishing Company, 101
Trivett, Abe, 10
Tubb, Ernest, 76–78, 94, 97
Turner, Ike, 104

Union Harmony (Caldwell), 12
Upson, Dean, 66

Vagabonds, 66
Vance, Fiddlin' Dudley, 46
Vaughan Brothers, 98
Vaughan, James D., music publishers, **51**, 52, 54
Veach, Rachel, **71**
Victor Company, 43, 100

Wagoner, Porter, 103, 109
Walker, Cas, 85–**87**, 88
Ward Company, 41
Waring's Pennsylvanians, 27
Warmack, Paul, **68**, 69
Waters, Margaret, 70
Watson, Doc, 47, **108**
WBAP (Ft. Worth), 55
WCYB (Bristol), 90
WDAD (Nashville), 55

WDOD (Chattanooga), 54
Webster Brothers, 88
Webster, J. P., 7
Weems String Band, 52
Weems, Ted, 97
Wells, Kitty, **87**, 94, 97, 103
West, Dottie, 103
Western Harmony, 12
Western Kentucky choking style (guitar), 100
Western swing, 70
Wexler, Jerry, 81
Wheeler, Onie, 60
White and King (*Sacred Harp*), 12
White, Lasses, 66, 70
Whiteman, Paul, 27
White Spirituals in the Southern Uplands (Jackson), 11
Whitter, Henry, 46
Whitter's Virginia Breakdowners, 41
Wiggins, Roy, 80
Wilds, Honey, 70
Wilkerson, G. W., 61
Williams, Hank, 77–78, 99, 104
Willis Brothers, 109
Wills, Bob, 75, 77, 78
Wills, Johnnie Lee, 96
Wilson, Edna, 70
Wilson, Frank, 42
Wilson, Lonnie (Pap), **70**
Wilson, Woodrow, 3
Wise, Chubby, **83**, 84
"The Wizard of Oz," 74
WJHL (Johnson City), 88
WJY (New York), 28
WLAC (Nashville), 50, 96
WLS (Chicago), 48, 54–55
WLW (Cincinnati), 48
WMC (Memphis), 54
WNOX (Knoxville), 54, 80, 85–86
WOAN (Lawrenceburg), 52, 54
Wood, Del, 103
Woodland studios, **108**
WOPI (Bristol), 80, **89**, 90
World Records, 96
Wright, Johnnie, 86, **87**
WROL (Knoxville), 73, 85–86, 88
WSB (Atlanta), 55
WSM (Nashville), 50, 55, 56, 59–60, 64, 67, 93–94, 101, 109
WTJS (Jackson, Tenn.), 78
Wynette, Tammy, 103

Young, Alvin, 49
Young, Jess, and his Tennessee Band, 49–50

INVENTORY 1983